Bipolar Women:

Thriving in the Ups and Downs

By

Sarah Rutledge

Disclaimer

The information presented in this book is for general educational purposes only and should not be construed as medical advice, diagnosis, or treatment. Always consult with a qualified healthcare professional regarding any questions or concerns you may have about your own or someone else's health. This book does not claim to provide a complete solution or cure for bipolar disorder, and individual experiences may vary.

While the author has made every effort to ensure the accuracy and completeness of the information provided, please note that medical knowledge and best practices are constantly evolving. This book is intended to be a starting point for your own research and should not be relied upon as the sole source of information.

Copyright Page

About the Author

In the pages of "Bipolar Women: Thriving in the Ups and Downs," you'll find an invaluable guide to understanding, managing, and living well with bipolar disorder. But before we delve into the rich tapestry of insights and strategies within these pages, let's take a moment to meet the brilliant mind behind this transformative work.

Our author,
Sarah is no stranger to the challenges of bipolar disorder. In fact, she's intimately acquainted with the rollercoaster of emotions, the dizzying highs, and the crushing lows that come with this often-misunderstood condition. Sarah's personal experience with bipolar disorder forms the foundation of her expertise, providing a unique perspective that is both relatable and enlightening.

Raised in a small town with big dreams, Sarah was a force to be reckoned with from an early age. She excelled academically, always hungry for knowledge and eager to unravel the complexities of the human mind. Little did she know that her own mind held secrets waiting to be unlocked.

As she navigated her teenage years, Sarah found herself grappling with an array of emotions that seemed to have a life of their own. One day, she would soar through the sky, bursting with creativity and energy, ready to conquer the world. The next, she would find herself sinking into a dark abyss, plagued by sadness and despair. It was during these tumultuous times that she discovered the name for her experiences - bipolar disorder.

Determined to take control of her own narrative, Sarah embarked on a journey of self-discovery and healing. She devoured books, attended therapy sessions, and sought out support groups. Through trial and error, she developed coping mechanisms, honed her management skills, and discovered a resilience within herself that she never knew existed.

But Sarah's journey didn't end there. Instead of keeping her newfound wisdom to herself, she made it her mission to share her experiences and knowledge with others. Recognizing the lack of resources specifically tailored to women with bipolar disorder, she decided to write the book she wished she had when she was first diagnosed.

And so, "Bipolar Women: Thriving in the Ups and Downs" was born. Within its pages, Sarah combines her personal anecdotes, clinical research, and expert advice to create a comprehensive guide that empowers women not just to survive but thrive with bipolar disorder. She tackles everything from managing medications and building a support network to navigating relationships and harnessing creativity. With a touch of humor and a generous sprinkling of wisdom, Sarah brings a ray of hope to every woman who has ever felt lost in the labyrinth of bipolar disorder.

Now, as you embark on your own journey through these pages, remember that you are not alone. Sarah's story and the stories of countless other women who have battled bipolar disorder are here to remind you that you have the strength within you to conquer anything that comes your way. So, buckle up, my friends, and get ready for an adventure like no other. Let's dive into the wild and wonderful world of bipolar disorder, where the ups and downs may be challenging, but the rewards are immeasurable.

Remember, if life hands you lemons, squeeze them into your iced tea and laugh in the face of adversity. After all, humor is the best medicine. And with Sarah as your guide, you'll be laughing your way to a brighter tomorrow in no time.

So, without further ado, let's turn the page and begin this extraordinary journey together. Welcome to the world of "Bipolar Women: Thriving in the Ups and Downs," - where understanding, managing, and living well with bipolar disorder is not just a possibility but a reality waiting to be embraced.

PREFACE

Picture this: You're on a roller coaster, the wind whipping through your hair, the adrenaline coursing through your veins. You're soaring high, feeling invincible, and nothing can bring you down. But suddenly, the ride takes a sharp turn, hurtling you down into the depths of despair. Your heart races, your mind spins, and you can't catch your breath. This is what it's like to have bipolar disorder. Bipolar disorder, also known as manic-depressive illness, is a mental health condition that affects millions of people worldwide. It's like having two extreme personalities living inside you, constantly at odds with each other. One moment, you're on top of the world, bursting with energy and ideas. The next, you're plunged into a darkness so deep that it feels impossible to escape. So, what are the symptoms of bipolar disorder? Well, it's not as simple as just feeling happy one moment and sad the next. Bipolar disorder is characterized by distinct episodes of mania and depression. During a manic episode, you might feel euphoric, full of grandiose ideas, and have an almost superhuman level of energy. You might talk a mile a minute, take on multiple projects at once, and have difficulty sleeping. It's like your brain is running on overdrive, and there's no off switch. On the other hand, a depressive episode feels like being trapped in a deep, dark hole with no way out. You might feel hopeless and lethargic and have a complete lack of interest in things that used to bring you joy. Simple tasks like getting out of bed or taking a shower become monumental challenges. It's like your world has been drained of color, and all you see is shades of gray. Now, you might be wondering, what causes bipolar disorder? Well, the exact cause is still unknown, but researchers believe it's a combination of genetic, biological, and environmental factors. It's like a perfect storm brewing inside your brain, waiting for the right trigger to set it off. It could be a stressful life event, a sudden change in routine, or even something as seemingly harmless as a change in sleep patterns. Diagnosing bipolar disorder can be a tricky business. After all, everyone has ups and downs. But when these ups and downs start interfering with your daily life, that's when it's time to seek help. A mental health professional will conduct a thorough evaluation, taking into account your symptoms, medical history, and family history. They might also ask you to keep a mood journal, tracking your emotions and behaviors over a period of time. Once diagnosed, it's important to remember that bipolar disorder is a chronic illness, but it's not a death sentence. With the right treatment plan, support system, and a dash of humor, you can learn to manage and thrive with bipolar disorder. It's like learning to ride that roller coaster with finesse, embracing the twists and turns, and finding joy in the ride. So, buckle up, my friend, because we're about to embark on a journey through the highs and lows of bipolar disorder. Together, we'll explore the intricacies of this condition, delve into the science behind it, and discover practical strategies for living well. And don't worry, I'll be right here with you, holding your hand and cracking a few jokes along the way. After all, laughter is the best medicine, right?

Table of Contents

CHAPTER 1:
Prevalence in Women

When it comes to bipolar disorder, it's important to recognize that women and men can experience the condition differently. There are certain factors that make women more prone to bipolar disorder, and understanding these differences can help in effectively managing and living well with the condition. One of the key reasons why bipolar disorder affects women differently than men is the hormonal fluctuations that occur throughout their lives. Let's face it, ladies, our hormones can be like a rollercoaster ride at times - up, down, and all around! And unfortunately, these hormonal shifts can have a significant impact on our mental health. Take puberty, for example. As if dealing with acne and awkward growth spurts wasn't enough, our bodies are also experiencing a surge of hormones during this time. And research has shown that this hormonal imbalance can trigger the onset of bipolar disorder in some women. It's like getting a double whammy - not fair! But the hormonal challenges don't stop there, my friends. Oh no, we have to deal with the joys of menstruation, too. Every month, like clockwork, our hormones go on a wild ride, wreaking havoc on our emotions and mental well-being. It's like having a permanent guest on the emotional rollercoaster, and it's no wonder that these fluctuations can exacerbate the symptoms of bipolar disorder. Pregnancy is another time when women are particularly vulnerable to the effects of bipolar disorder. The surge of hormones during pregnancy can cause a whirlwind of emotions and mood swings, which can be challenging to navigate for anyone, let alone someone with bipolar disorder. And let's not forget the postpartum period - the joy of welcoming a new bundle of joy is often accompanied by sleep deprivation, hormonal changes, and the infamous baby blues. For women with bipolar disorder, this can be a recipe for a serious mental health storm. Now, don't get me wrong, ladies. It's not all doom and gloom. We're strong, resilient beings, and we have the power to thrive despite these challenges. But it's essential to recognize and address the unique ways that bipolar disorder affects us. By understanding the prevalence of bipolar disorder in women and the factors that contribute to these differences, we can better manage our condition. It's about finding a balance, like walking a tightrope without falling off (and yes, I'm talking about both the hormonal tightrope and the mental health tightrope!). So, how can we do this? Well, education is key. Understanding our bodies, our hormones, and the ways in which they interact with bipolar disorder can empower us to make informed decisions about our mental health. We can work with healthcare professionals to develop personalized treatment plans that take into account our unique needs as women. Additionally, finding support is crucial. We are not alone in this journey, my friends. Connecting with others who have experienced similar challenges can provide a sense of camaraderie and understanding. And let's be real: having a tribe of badass bipolar women who can relate to your struggles and share a laugh (or a cry) with you is priceless. So, ladies, let's embrace our unique experiences with bipolar disorder. We may have to deal with hormonal rollercoasters and the occasional mood swings, but we are resilient. We are capable of thriving in the ups and downs. And with a little knowledge, support, and maybe a chocolate bar or two, we can navigate this journey with grace and humor. After all, laughter is the best medicine, right?

Impact on Relationships

Relationships can be a rollercoaster ride, even in the best of times. Throw bipolar disorder into the mix, and you've got a ride that could rival the wildest theme park attractions. Bipolar disorder has a way of impacting personal relationships, and if not managed properly, it can send those connections careening off the tracks. But fear not, my dear reader, for in this chapter, we will explore the impact of bipolar disorder on relationships and equip you with strategies to keep those connections thriving. When it comes to bipolar disorder, one of the most significant challenges lies in the unpredictable nature of the condition. The ups and downs, the highs and lows, can create a whirlwind of emotions that can be difficult for both the individual with bipolar disorder and their loved ones to navigate. One moment, you're basking in the glow of the person's infectious energy and zest for life, and the next, you find yourself caught in the eye of the storm, wondering where that person you know and love has gone. It's important to remember that bipolar disorder doesn't define a person's entire being. It's just one piece of the puzzle, albeit a significant one. Understanding this is crucial in maintaining healthy connections. Instead of solely focusing on the disorder, it's essential to see the person behind it – the person with hopes, dreams, and a beautiful soul. Communication is the key to any successful relationship, and this holds even more weight when bipolar disorder is involved. Open, honest, and compassionate communication can help bridge the gap between understanding and confusion. Encourage your loved one to express their feelings and concerns and be prepared to do the same. And remember, my friend, a good laugh can go a long way. When discussing difficult topics, a well-timed joke can break the tension and remind you both that you're in this together, facing life's challenges side by side. Another strategy for maintaining healthy connections is to educate yourself about bipolar disorder. Arm yourself with knowledge, my friend, for knowledge is power. Learn about the symptoms, the triggers, and the treatment options. Understand that bipolar disorder is a complex condition, and it affects everyone differently. By educating yourself, you can better support your loved one and navigate the turbulent waters of their emotional landscape. Patience is a virtue, they say, and never has this been truer than when it comes to bipolar disorder and relationships. The highs and lows may come and go, but your love and support can remain steadfast. Remember that the person you care about is not their illness; they are a beautiful soul deserving of compassion and understanding. So, my friend, take a deep breath, count to ten if you must, and remind yourself that you're in this for the long haul. It's also essential to take care of yourself, for you cannot pour from an empty cup. Supporting someone with bipolar disorder can be emotionally taxing, and it's vital that you prioritize your own well-being. Set boundaries, seek support from friends and family, and engage in self-care activities that bring you joy and replenish your spirit. In conclusion, bipolar disorder can undoubtedly impact personal relationships, but it doesn't have to be the end of the world. With open communication, education, patience, and self-care, you can maintain healthy connections and thrive in the face of adversity. Remember, my dear reader, love knows no bounds, and together, you and your loved one can conquer the ups and downs of bipolar disorder, hand in hand, heart to heart. And if all else fails, well, a good laugh and a cheesy joke never hurt anyone. Why did the bipolar bear become a comedian? Because laughter is the best medicine, my friend, even for the wildest rollercoaster rides.

Stigma and Misconceptions

Addressing Common Misconceptions and Stigma Surrounding Bipolar Disorder in Women

In the realm of mental health, bipolar disorder is often misunderstood and stigmatized. This is especially true for women who are living with this condition. While the topic may seem daunting, it's important to address the common misconceptions and stigma surrounding bipolar disorder in women head-on. By doing so, we can foster understanding and support and ultimately help women thrive in the ups and downs of their lives. So, let's dive into this often-misunderstood world and shed light on the truth behind the misconceptions.

Misconception 1: Women with bipolar disorder are unpredictable and dangerous.

Ah, the age-old stereotype of the "crazy woman." It's time to debunk this misconception once and for all. While it's true that bipolar disorder can lead to mood swings, it doesn't automatically make women dangerous or unpredictable. In fact, many women with bipolar disorder are incredibly self-aware and work diligently to manage their symptoms. So, the next time you encounter someone who says, "She has bipolar disorder, so you never know what she'll do," kindly remind them that the majority of women with bipolar disorder are just like anyone else – kind, compassionate, and fully capable of leading fulfilling lives.

Misconception 2: Women with bipolar disorder are incapable of maintaining healthy relationships.

This misconception couldn't be further from the truth. Yes, bipolar disorder presents unique challenges when it comes to relationships, but with proper management and support, women with bipolar disorder can maintain healthy and fulfilling connections. It's all about communication, understanding, and a little bit of patience. So, the next time you hear someone say, "I could never date someone with bipolar disorder," gently remind them that love and understanding can conquer any obstacle, including mental health conditions.

Misconception 3: Women with bipolar disorder are always in a manic or depressive state.

Contrary to popular belief, bipolar disorder doesn't mean a constant rollercoaster ride of extreme emotions. In reality, there are periods of stability and balance for individuals with bipolar disorder. This misconception often stems from media portrayals that sensationalize the extremes, neglecting to show the everyday experiences of those living with bipolar disorder. So, the next time someone says, "She must be in a manic phase," educate them about the complexities of bipolar disorder and how it can manifest differently in each individual.

Misconception 4: Women with bipolar disorder cannot lead successful and fulfilling lives.

Ah, the misconception that breaks our hearts. Women with bipolar disorder are capable of achieving incredible success and finding fulfillment in their lives. It's important to remember that mental health conditions do not define a person's worth or potential. By sharing stories of resilience, creativity, and accomplishment, we can inspire others and break down the barriers of stigma. So, the next time you encounter someone who believes that women with bipolar disorder are destined for a life of struggle, share stories of women who have defied the odds and are thriving in their personal and professional lives.

Addressing Stigma:

Now that we've addressed some of the common misconceptions surrounding bipolar disorder in women let's talk about the stigma that often accompanies this condition. Stigma can manifest in various ways, from discriminatory attitudes to social exclusion. It's crucial to address and combat this stigma to create a more inclusive and understanding society.

Education is key. By increasing awareness and providing accurate information about bipolar disorder, we can dispel myths and misconceptions. Let's encourage open conversations about mental health, where individuals feel safe to share their experiences without fear of judgment.

Support networks are vital. Women living with bipolar disorder often benefit from connecting with others who can relate to their experiences. Support groups, online communities, and therapy can provide a sense of belonging and validation. Together, we can create a supportive environment where women with bipolar disorder feel empowered to seek help and support.

Challenging language and stereotypes. Words have power, and the language we use can perpetuate stigma or challenge it. Let's move away from derogatory labels and instead focus on compassionate and inclusive language when discussing mental health conditions. By doing so, we create a safe space for individuals to seek help and feel understood.

In conclusion, addressing the common misconceptions and stigma surrounding bipolar disorder in women is a crucial step toward creating a more compassionate and supportive society. By promoting understanding, empathy, and accurate information, we can empower women with bipolar disorder to thrive in their lives, embracing both the ups and downs with resilience and strength. So, let's challenge the misconceptions, break down the barriers, and pave the way for a world where every woman can live well with bipolar disorder. Remember, together, we can make a difference – one stigma at a time.

And now, to lighten the mood, here's a little joke for you: Why did the bipolar woman bring a ladder to the bar? She was ready for the highs and lows of the night! Remember, laughter is often the best medicine, even when addressing serious topics.

Seeking Professional Help

Seeking Professional Help: Guiding You to the Right Healthcare Providers and the Importance of a Comprehensive Treatment Plan

In the journey of managing bipolar disorder, seeking professional help is like finding the perfect pair of shoes - it may take some time and a few blisters, but once you find the right fit, it can make all the difference. In this chapter, we will explore the importance of finding the right healthcare providers and the value of a comprehensive treatment plan. So, grab your metaphorical magnifying glass, and let's embark on this investigative journey together!

When it comes to finding healthcare providers, it's crucial to remember that you are the detective in charge of your own mental health case. It's easy to feel overwhelmed by the sheer number of psychiatrists, therapists, and other professionals out there. But fear not, dear reader, for I have a few tricks up my sleeve to help you navigate this maze.

First and foremost, it's essential to find professionals who specialize in bipolar disorder. Think of it this way: you wouldn't go to a dentist for a broken bone, would you? Well, the same logic applies here. Seek out experts who have extensive knowledge and experience in treating bipolar disorder. They'll know the ins and outs of the condition and the latest treatment options and can tailor their approach to suit your unique needs.

Now, you may be wondering, "But how do I find these unicorn-like professionals?" Fear not, for I shall guide you through the wilderness of online directories and recommendations. Start by asking for referrals from your primary care physician, friends, or support groups. Word-of-mouth recommendations can be like gold in the realm of mental healthcare. If that doesn't yield any leads, turn to trusted online resources that specialize in mental health provider directories. These directories often include detailed profiles, reviews, and ratings to help you make an informed decision.

Once you've gathered a list of potential providers, it's time to put your detective skills to the test. Schedule an initial consultation with each of them, treating it like a detective's interrogation (minus the trench coat and fedora). Come prepared with a list of questions that delve into their expertise, treatment approach, and what they had for breakfast (okay, maybe not the last one). This meeting is your chance to assess their compatibility with your needs, gauge their communication style, and see if they have a sense of humor that matches your own. After all, laughter can be the best medicine, especially when life throws you a bipolar-shaped curveball.

Now, let's shift gears and talk about the importance of a comprehensive treatment plan. Picture it as a roadmap guiding you through the winding roads of bipolar disorder. Just as you wouldn't embark on a cross-country road trip without a GPS, you shouldn't navigate your mental health journey without a well-crafted plan.

A comprehensive treatment plan involves a multi-pronged approach that encompasses medication, therapy, self-care, and support systems. It's like assembling a superhero team, with each member playing a vital role in your well-being. The medication acts as a powerful shield, reducing the intensity of mood swings. Therapy becomes the wise sage, helping you uncover the root causes of your struggles and equipping you with coping strategies. Self-care serves as the trusty sidekick, reminding you to prioritize your mental and physical health. And your support system? Well, they're the Avengers, standing by your side when things get tough.

Remember, dear reader, that a comprehensive treatment plan is not a one-size-fits-all solution. It's an evolving masterpiece crafted specifically for you and your unique journey. Adjustments will be made, and detours may be taken, but with each step, you'll be inching closer to a life of stability and fulfillment.

Now, I know what you're thinking - "This all sounds great, but how do I stay motivated when the going gets tough?" Ah, my dear reader, let me share a secret weapon with you - the power of humor. Laughter has the incredible ability to ease tension, brighten even the darkest of days, and remind us that we're not alone in this bipolar rollercoaster ride. So, don't be afraid to sprinkle some humor into your treatment plan. Whether it's finding joy in the little things, cracking jokes with your therapist, or indulging in a good old-fashioned comedy show, humor can be a powerful tool in your arsenal.

In conclusion, dear reader, seeking professional help is a critical step in your bipolar journey. By finding the right healthcare providers and crafting a comprehensive treatment plan, you'll be equipping yourself with the tools and support needed to thrive in the ups and downs of bipolar disorder. So, put on your detective hat, embrace your sense of humor, and let the journey toward mental wellness begin!

Remember, my dear reader, you're the hero of this story. And with the right support and a dash of humor, you'll conquer every twist and turn that bipolar disorder throws your way. Stay strong, stay resilient, and most importantly, stay hopeful. The road may be bumpy, but you have everything you need to thrive in the ups and downs of life with bipolar disorder. Keep seeking help, keep crafting that comprehensive treatment plan, and always remember - you are not alone.

Chapter 2:
Understanding Bipolar Disorder

Different Types of Bipolar Disorder

When it comes to bipolar disorder, it's not a one-size-fits-all kind of situation. Oh no, my friends, there are different types of this wild ride called bipolar disorder, each with its own unique characteristics. It's like going to a theme park and trying out all the different roller coasters – except these roller coasters are happening inside your brain. Fun, right? Well, maybe not always, but we're here to explore these various subtypes and shed some light on what makes them special.

First up, we have good old bipolar I disorder. This is the granddaddy of them all, the one that gets all the attention. It's like the front-row seat on a roller coaster – you get to experience the highest highs and the lowest lows. With bipolar I, you might find yourself soaring to the heights of mania, feeling like you can conquer the world. But watch out because those manic episodes can quickly turn into a downward spiral of depression. It's a wild ride, my friends, but at least you'll never be bored.

Next, we have bipolar II disorder. Think of this as the roller coaster in the middle – not as intense as the front row, but still enough to get your heart racing. With bipolar II, you'll experience hypomania, which is like a watered-down version of full-blown mania. It's like having a shot of espresso without the sugar rush. You'll feel energized, creative, and maybe a little impulsive. But don't worry, because after the hypomania comes the crash into depression. It's like the post-coffee crash but on a whole other level.

Now, let's talk about cyclothymic disorder. This one's like the kiddie coaster at the theme park – it's not as extreme, but it still has its ups and downs. With cyclothymic disorder, you'll experience milder versions of mania and depression, but they'll still be enough to make you feel like you're on a wild ride. It's like the teacup ride that spins you around and around – you'll feel dizzy and disoriented, but at least it's not as intense as the big roller coasters.

And finally, we have rapid-cycling bipolar disorder. This one's like being on a roller coaster that never stops. With rapid cycling, you'll experience four or more episodes of mania, hypomania, or depression within a year. It's like being on the world's longest roller coaster – you're constantly going up and down, up and down. It can be exhausting, but hey, at least you'll never have a dull moment.

So, there you have it, folks – the different types of bipolar disorder. Each one has its own unique characteristics and its own ups and downs. It's like having a whole theme park inside your brain. But remember, just like at a theme park, there are ways to manage and enjoy the ride. Medication, therapy, and a solid support system can make all the difference. And hey, a sense of humor doesn't hurt either. So, buckle up, my friends, and get ready for the ride of your life. It may be a wild one, but with the right tools and a dash of laughter, you can thrive in the ups and downs of bipolar disorder.

Symptoms and Warning Signs

In the tumultuous sea of emotions that is bipolar disorder, women often find themselves navigating treacherous waves that threaten to engulf them. But fear not, dear reader, for in this segment, we shall explore the common symptoms and warning signs of bipolar disorder in women. So grab your life vest, and let's dive in!

The Ups and Downs of Bipolar Disorder:

Picture this: you're riding the roller coaster of life, but instead of being confined to the tracks, you find yourself hurtling through the clouds one moment and plunging into the depths of despair the next. Welcome to the world of bipolar disorder. This mental health condition is characterized by extreme mood swings, ranging from the highs of mania to the lows of depression. And women, oh, how they can dance between these extremes with a finesse that would make even the most seasoned tightrope walker envious.

The Manic Marvels:

Ah, the exhilaration of a manic episode! It's like strapping yourself to a rocket ship and blasting off into a universe where sleep is optional and ideas flow faster than a river in spring. During these manic episodes, women with bipolar disorder may exhibit a range of symptoms, such as heightened energy levels, racing thoughts, an inflated sense of self-importance, and a penchant for taking on multiple projects at once. It's like having a thousand tabs open in your brain, except you're the one who opened them all!

The Depressive Depths:

But what goes up must come down, and when it comes to bipolar disorder, the descent into depression can be a harrowing experience. Women with bipolar disorder may find themselves trapped in a fog of sadness, hopelessness, and an overwhelming fatigue that makes even the simplest tasks feel like climbing Mount Everest. It's like being stuck in a never-ending rainstorm with no umbrella in sight.

The Mixed Bag:

Just when you thought you had bipolar disorder all figured out, it throws you a curveball in the form of a mixed episode. Imagine feeling the energy of mania coursing through your veins but with the darkness of depression weighing you down like a lead balloon. Women experiencing a mixed episode may find themselves restless, agitated, and prone to impulsive behavior. It's like trying to dance the tango while wearing roller skates - a thrilling yet precarious balancing act.

The Red Flags:

Now that we've explored the wild terrain of bipolar disorder, let's shine a spotlight on the warning signs that may signal its presence. Women with bipolar disorder may experience changes in sleep patterns, appetite, and concentration. They may also exhibit irritability, racing thoughts, and a loss of interest in activities they once enjoyed. It's like having a neon sign flashing "Something's not quite right!" in the back of your mind.

Seeking Help and Support:

Remember, dear reader, you are not alone in this journey. There are lifelines available to help you navigate the turbulent waters of bipolar disorder. Seeking professional help from a mental health expert is essential, as they can provide a diagnosis, develop a treatment plan, and offer invaluable support. Additionally, reaching out to friends, family, and support groups can provide a lifeline of understanding and empathy. Together, we can weather the storm and emerge stronger than ever before.

In the symphony of life, bipolar disorder adds an unexpected melody that can be both beautiful and challenging. By highlighting the common symptoms and warning signs of bipolar disorder in women, we hope to shed light on this often-misunderstood condition. So, dear reader, may you embrace your ups and downs with grace, find strength in your journey, and thrive in the face of adversity. And remember, when life hands your lemons, make a deliciously tart lemonade spiked with resilience and a splash of humor. Cheers to thriving in the ups and downs of bipolar disorder!

Triggers and Risk Factors

In order to truly understand and manage bipolar disorder, it is crucial to identify the triggers and risk factors that can contribute to its onset and exacerbation. These factors can vary from person to person, but they often fall into three main categories: environmental, genetic, and lifestyle. Let's take a closer look at each of these factors, shall we?

Firstly, let's talk about the environmental triggers. These are the external factors that can potentially disrupt the delicate balance of the brain and lead to the manifestation of bipolar symptoms. Stress, for instance, is a notorious trigger that can send our moods spiraling in either direction. Whether it's work-related stress, relationship troubles, or even just the demands of daily life, stress has a knack for pushing our emotional buttons. But fear not! Remember, stress is like a blender without a lid - it may splatter everywhere, but with a little mindfulness, you can keep it contained.

Next up, we have the genetic factors. Bipolar disorder has a strong genetic component, meaning that if you have a family member with the condition, your risk of developing it is significantly higher. Now, I know what you're thinking - "Great, I won the genetic lottery!" But fear not, my friend, because genetics are only part of the equation. It's like having a loaded gun; it doesn't necessarily mean you'll pull the trigger. Understanding your genetic predisposition can actually be empowering. It allows you to be proactive in managing your mental health and implementing strategies to prevent triggers from taking control.

Last but not least, we have lifestyle factors. These are the choices we make in our day-to-day lives that can either fuel the fire or douse the flames of bipolar disorder. Sleep, for instance, plays a pivotal role in maintaining stability. Without enough sleep, our mood can resemble a rollercoaster ride on steroids. So, make sure to prioritize those Zzz's and create a bedtime routine that would make even the Sandman proud. And speaking of routines, having a consistent daily schedule can work wonders in managing bipolar symptoms. It's like having a roadmap for your day, ensuring you stay on track and avoid any detours into emotional turbulence.

Now, before we move on, let's take a moment to appreciate the absurdity of life. I mean, who would have thought that a disorder with such a serious impact on our lives would have triggers that sound like the ingredients for a wacky sitcom? Stress, genetics, and sleep - it's like the start of a bad joke. But here's the punchline: by understanding and addressing these triggers, we can take back control and thrive in the face of bipolar disorder.

So, my fellow bipolar warriors, take a deep breath, embrace your uniqueness, and remember that life is a comedy, not a tragedy. By identifying and managing these triggers and risk factors, you are equipped with the tools to live well and thrive in the ups and downs of bipolar disorder. And hey, if all else fails, remember that laughter truly is the best medicine. So go ahead, find the humor in life's quirks, and let your spirit soar. After all, a little laughter can go a long way in keeping those moods in check. Keep on thriving, my friends!

Comorbidities and Dual Diagnosis

Examining the Connection Between Bipolar Disorder and Other Mental Health Conditions

Picture this: You're sitting in a crowded waiting room, nervously fidgeting with your appointment reminder. The clock on the wall is moving at a snail's pace as if time itself is playing a cruel joke on you. Finally, the door opens, and you are called in to meet your psychiatrist. As you enter the room, you can't help but notice the stacks of medical textbooks piled high on the shelves, each one seemingly thicker than the last. You take a deep breath and prepare yourself for what lies ahead – the daunting task of unraveling the complex web of comorbidities and dual diagnosis.

Comorbidities, as the name suggests, refer to the presence of two or more medical conditions occurring simultaneously in an individual. In the realm of mental health, comorbidities can be like unexpected guests crashing a party just when you thought you had bipolar disorder to contend with, in walks anxiety, depression, or substance abuse. It's as if life decided to throw a curveball your way to keep things interesting. But fear not! Understanding the connection between bipolar disorder and these comorbid conditions can shed light on the path to managing and living well with this challenging disorder.

Let's start with anxiety. If bipolar disorder were a rollercoaster ride, anxiety would be the tightrope you walk while on it. The constant worry, the racing thoughts, the gnawing feeling in the pit of your stomach – these are all familiar companions to those with bipolar disorder. It's like having a battle royale between your mind and body, each one vying for dominance. But here's the twist: anxiety can actually be a symptom of bipolar disorder itself, or it can be a separate condition that happens to tag along for the ride. Either way, it's important to address anxiety head-on because, let's face it, nobody wants to be on the edge of their seat all the time – unless they're at a thrilling movie or a stand-up comedy show.

Moving on to depression, it's like the rainy days that follow a thunderstorm. Bipolar disorder already takes you on a wild ride, swinging from the highs of mania to the lows of depression. But when depression decides to cozy up and make itself at home, it's like adding insult to injury. You may find yourself feeling down, hopeless, and lacking the energy to even get out of bed in the morning. But fear not, my friend, for there is hope! Understanding the interplay between bipolar disorder and depression can help you navigate through the stormy seas and find the silver lining in even the darkest of clouds.

Now, let's address the elephant in the room – substance abuse. It's like a mischievous imp that sneaks its way into your life, wreaking havoc along the way. Bipolar disorder and substance abuse often go hand in hand, like the proverbial peanut butter and jelly. Many individuals with bipolar disorder turn to drugs or alcohol as a way to self-medicate, numb the pain, or escape the relentless rollercoaster of emotions. But here's the catch: substance abuse not only exacerbates the symptoms of bipolar disorder, but it can also interfere with the effectiveness of medications and treatment. It's like pouring gasoline on a fire, hoping it will put it out – it's just not going to work. So, my friend, put down that shot glass or that pack of cigarettes, and let's embark on a journey toward a healthier, happier you.

The connection between bipolar disorder and other mental health conditions is like a tangled web that requires careful unraveling. By understanding the intricacies of comorbidities and dual diagnosis, you can better equip yourself with the tools to manage and live well with bipolar disorder. Remember, you are not alone in this journey. Seek support, whether it be from mental health professionals, support groups, or trusted friends and family. And above all, never lose sight of the fact that you have the strength and resilience to thrive in the ups and downs of life. So, my friend, hold on tight – it's going to be one heck of a ride!

And hey, remember that old saying: "Laugh in the face of adversity." So, here's a little joke to lighten the mood:

Why did the bipolar bear go to therapy?

Because he was tired of feeling bipolar – he wanted to be a pro-polar!

Okay, okay, I know it's a cheesy joke, but hey, laughter is the best medicine, right? So, my friend, keep smiling, keep learning, and keep thriving. You've got this!

Managing Mood Episodes

Living with bipolar disorder can often feel like a rollercoaster ride, with its ups and downs, twists and turns. One moment, you may find yourself soaring high with energy, creativity, and confidence, while the next, you may plummet into a deep and dark abyss of depression and despair. These extreme mood swings, known as manic and depressive episodes, can be incredibly challenging to navigate. But fear not, for in this chapter, we will explore practical strategies for managing these mood episodes and finding stability amidst the chaos.

Let's start with manic episodes. Picture this: you're feeling on top of the world, like you could conquer anything and everything. You have a million ideas racing through your mind, and you can't seem to slow down. While it may be tempting to embrace this surge of energy and productivity, it's crucial to maintain a balance. One strategy is to channel your manic energy into productive outlets, such as creative projects or physical activities. Paint a masterpiece, write a novel, or run a marathon – the possibilities are endless! Just remember to pace yourself and avoid overexertion, as it can lead to burnout.

Now, let's switch gears and talk about depressive episodes. Imagine waking up one morning and feeling like you're carrying the weight of the world on your shoulders. Everything feels hopeless, and even the simplest tasks seem insurmountable. In these moments, it's important to practice self-care and reach out for support. Surround yourself with a strong support network of friends, family, and mental health professionals who can offer a listening ear and a helping hand. Engage in activities that bring you joy, whether it's cuddling up with a good book, going for a walk-in nature, or indulging in some retail therapy (within reason, of course!).

Another strategy for managing both manic and depressive episodes is to establish a routine. Bipolar disorder often disrupts our natural circadian rhythms, leading to erratic sleep patterns and irregular daily routines. By setting a consistent schedule for sleep, meals, Exercise, and medication, you can provide a sense of stability and structure in your life. It may take some trial and error to find a routine that works for you, but once you do, stick to it like glue—well, maybe not as sticky as glue, but you get the point!

In addition to routine, it's crucial to prioritize self-awareness and self-monitoring. Learn to recognize the early warning signs of both manic and depressive episodes. Are you sleeping less, talking faster, and engaging in impulsive behaviors? These may be indicators of an impending manic episode. On the other hand, if you find yourself sleeping excessively, feeling fatigued, and withdrawing from activities you once enjoyed, it may be a sign of depression creeping in. By being attuned to these warning signs, you can take proactive measures to manage your mood episodes before they spiral out of control.

Of course, managing mood episodes is not a one-size-fits-all approach. Each person's experience with bipolar disorder is unique, and what works for one may not work for another. It's important to consult with a mental health professional who can tailor a treatment plan specifically for you. Medication, therapy, and lifestyle adjustments can all play a role in managing your mood episodes effectively. Remember, you are not alone in this journey, and with the right support and strategies, you can thrive in the ups and downs of bipolar disorder.

Now, before we wrap up this chapter, let me leave you with a little joke to lighten the mood. Why did the bipolar bear bring a ladder to the party? Because he wanted to reach new heights – both literally and metaphorically! Okay, maybe that was a bit cheesy, but humor has its way of bringing a smile to our faces, even in the darkest of times.

So, dear reader, as you continue on your path of managing mood episodes, remember to be kind to yourself, stay resilient, and embrace the journey of living well with bipolar disorder. You are capable, you are strong, and you have the power to thrive in the ups and downs.

Chapter 3:
Building a Support System

Family and Friends

Advising on How to Educate Loved Ones about Bipolar Disorder and Involve Them in the Recovery Process

As we navigate the ups and downs of bipolar disorder, one thing becomes abundantly clear - we can't do it alone. Our family and friends play a crucial role in our journey towards managing and thriving with this condition. However, sometimes, they might not fully understand what bipolar disorder entails or how they can support us effectively. That's why it's essential to educate our loved ones about bipolar disorder and involve them in our recovery process. So, please grab a cup of coffee, gather your family and friends around, and let's dive into some practical advice on how to make this happen.

First and foremost, it's essential to approach the topic with empathy, patience, and a touch of humor. Bipolar disorder can be a heavy subject, but sprinkling in some jokes can help lighten the mood and make it more approachable. For example, you could say something like, "Did you know that living with bipolar disorder is like riding a rollercoaster? Except, instead of cotton candy and a souvenir photo, you get mood swings and a medication schedule."

Now that you have their attention, it's time to educate them about bipolar disorder. Start by explaining the basics - what it is and how it affects you. Use simple, concrete language that they can easily understand. Imagine you're explaining it to a child but without sounding condescending. Remember, the goal is to provide them with a solid foundation of knowledge so they can better grasp what you're going through.

To help them understand the highs and lows of bipolar disorder, you can use metaphors and similes. For instance, you might say, "During a manic episode, it's like my brain becomes a racecar on a never-ending track, zooming from one thought to another at lightning speed. But during a depressive episode, it's like my brain turns into a cozy blanket fort on a rainy day, where it's hard to find the motivation to do anything."

Once they have a grasp of the basics, it's time to involve them in your recovery process. Explain the importance of support networks and how their presence and understanding can make a world of difference. Please encourage them to ask questions and express their concerns openly. This open line of communication will help foster a sense of trust and enable them to provide the support you need.

Additionally, consider inviting them to therapy sessions or support group meetings. This can be an eye-opening experience for them, as they witness firsthand the challenges you face and the strategies you employ to manage your condition. It also allows them to connect with others who may be going through similar experiences, further strengthening their understanding and empathy.

It's important to remember that educating loved ones about bipolar disorder is an ongoing process. Be patient with them and yourself, as it might take time for them to grasp the complexities of the condition fully. Please encourage them to continue learning and seeking out resources that can enhance their understanding.

In conclusion, involving our family and friends in our journey with bipolar disorder is vital for our overall well-being. By educating them about the condition and inviting them to be part of our recovery process, we create a support network that can make all the difference. So, next time you gather your loved ones around, armed with coffee and a few well-placed jokes, remember that you're not just informing them about bipolar disorder; you're inviting them to be an essential part of your thriving together.

Support Groups and Therapy

Support groups and therapy are two powerful tools that can greatly benefit individuals living with bipolar disorder. While it may be tempting to brush off these resources as unnecessary or ineffective, the truth is that they can play a pivotal role in managing and thriving with this condition. In this chapter, we will delve into the benefits of participating in support groups and therapy, shedding light on why they are so essential for individuals with bipolar disorder.

Let's start with support groups. Imagine a room filled with people who truly understand what you're going through—the highs, the lows, and everything in between. That's the beauty of support groups. These gatherings provide a safe and

+non-judgmental space for individuals with bipolar disorder to connect with others who share similar experiences. It's like having a tribe of people who "get it."

Support groups offer a multitude of benefits. Firstly, they help combat feelings of isolation and loneliness that often accompany bipolar disorder. When you're surrounded by a supportive community, you no longer feel like you're navigating this journey alone. You have people who can empathize with your struggles and offer genuine understanding and encouragement.

Additionally, support groups provide a platform for sharing coping strategies and tips for managing bipolar symptoms. Each person brings their unique perspective and experiences to the table, creating a rich pool of knowledge and wisdom. From practical advice on medication management to innovative self-care techniques, these groups become a treasure trove of information.

But it's not just about receiving support; it's also about giving it. By actively participating in support groups, individuals with bipolar disorder can offer their own insights and support to others. This act of helping and supporting others can be incredibly empowering and fulfilling, boosting self-esteem and fostering a sense of purpose.

Now, let's turn our attention to therapy. Therapy, whether it's individual or group-based, can be a game-changer for individuals with bipolar disorder. The therapeutic setting provides a safe and confidential space to explore thoughts, emotions, and behaviors with the guidance of a trained professional.

Therapy helps individuals with bipolar disorder develop essential coping skills and strategies to manage their symptoms effectively. Through various therapeutic techniques, such as cognitive-behavioral therapy (CBT) or dialectical behavior therapy (DBT), individuals learn to identify triggers, regulate their emotions, and develop healthy coping mechanisms.

One of the significant benefits of therapy is the opportunity to gain a deeper understanding of oneself and one's condition. By working closely with a therapist, individuals can uncover patterns and triggers that contribute to their bipolar symptoms. This newfound insight allows them to make informed choices and take proactive steps toward better mental health.

Therapy also provides a space for individuals to explore and address any underlying emotional or psychological issues that may be exacerbating their bipolar disorder. Sometimes, unresolved trauma or unresolved grief can significantly impact one's mental well-being. Therapy offers a safe container to process these emotions and work towards healing.

Now, you might be thinking, "But therapy is so serious! Is there any room for humor?" Absolutely! Humor can be a powerful tool in therapy, helping individuals lighten the mood and find some levity amidst the challenges they face. In fact, some therapists even use humor intentionally to create a more relaxed and comfortable atmosphere.

Imagine this scenario: you're sitting in therapy, discussing the ups and downs of bipolar disorder, when suddenly, your therapist cracks a well-timed joke. It catches you off guard, and you find yourself bursting into laughter. In that moment, the weight of your struggles feels a little lighter, and you realize that even in the darkest times, there can be moments of joy and laughter.

In conclusion, support groups and therapy offer invaluable benefits for individuals with bipolar disorder. They provide a sense of community, a wealth of knowledge, and a safe space to heal and grow. So, if you're living with bipolar disorder, don't hesitate to explore these resources. Embrace the power of connection and therapy, and take the first step towards living well with bipolar disorder. Remember, you don't have to face this journey alone. Together, we can thrive in the ups and downs of bipolar disorder!

Self-Care and Lifestyle Changes

Promoting self-care practices and lifestyle adjustments that can enhance overall well-being is an essential aspect of managing bipolar disorder. In this chapter, we will explore various strategies and techniques that can help individuals with bipolar disorder thrive in their daily lives.

Self-care is not a luxury; it is a necessity for individuals with bipolar disorder. It involves taking deliberate actions to improve one's physical, emotional, and mental well-being. One of the most crucial aspects of self-care is establishing a consistent daily routine. This routine should include regular sleep patterns, Exercise, and healthy eating habits.

Sleep is particularly vital for individuals with bipolar disorder, as disruptions in sleep can trigger mood swings. It's essential to prioritize getting enough sleep and maintaining a consistent sleep schedule. Avoiding caffeine and electronic devices before bedtime can also help promote better sleep.

Exercise is another important self-care practice that can have a significant impact on mood stability. Engaging in regular physical activity, whether it's going for a walk, practicing Yoga, or participating in a favorite sport, can help release endorphins, reduce stress, and improve overall well-being. Remember, Exercise doesn't have to be intense or time-consuming; even short bursts of activity can make a difference.

Eating a balanced and nutritious diet is also crucial for individuals with bipolar disorder. Certain foods, such as those rich in omega-3 fatty acids, can help reduce inflammation in the brain and improve mood. Incorporating foods like fatty fish, walnuts, and flaxseeds into your diet can provide these essential nutrients. Additionally, limiting the consumption of processed foods, sugar, and alcohol can help stabilize mood and improve overall health.

In addition to these self-care practices, there are lifestyle adjustments that can enhance the well-being of individuals with bipolar disorder. One such adjustment is the practice of stress management techniques. Stress can exacerbate symptoms of bipolar disorder, so finding healthy ways to manage and reduce stress is crucial. This could include activities such as meditation, deep breathing exercises, journaling, or engaging in hobbies that bring joy and relaxation.

Another lifestyle adjustment that can greatly impact overall well-being is the establishment of a strong support system. Surrounding oneself with understanding and supportive friends, family, or support groups can provide a sense of belonging and help individuals navigate the challenges of bipolar disorder. Being able to communicate about one's experiences and emotions openly can be incredibly empowering.

It's important to note that self-care and lifestyle adjustments are not a one-size-fits-all solution. Each individual with bipolar disorder is unique, and it may take some trial and error to find the strategies and practices that work best for you. Be patient with yourself and allow room for experimentation.

Promoting self-care practices and making lifestyle adjustments are essential components of managing bipolar disorder. By prioritizing sleep, Exercise, nutrition, stress management, and building a strong support system, individuals with bipolar disorder can enhance their overall well-being and thrive in their daily lives. So, embrace self-care, make those lifestyle changes, and let your inner light shine through the ups and downs of bipolar disorder!

The Role of Medication

One of the key components in managing bipolar disorder is medication. It plays a crucial role in stabilizing mood swings and reducing the intensity of manic and depressive episodes. But what exactly are these medications, and how do they work? Let's dive into the world of bipolar medication and explore the different types and potential side effects.

First up, we have mood stabilizers. These medications, as the name suggests, help to stabilize and regulate mood fluctuations. Lithium, for example, is a commonly prescribed mood stabilizer that has been used for decades. It's like the superhero of medications, swooping in to save the day and keep those manic and depressive episodes at bay. However, like any superhero, it does have some side effects. It can cause tremors and weight gain and even impact your thyroid function. But hey, it's a small price to pay for emotional stability, right?

Next on the list are antipsychotics. Now, don't let the name scare you. These medications are not about to turn you into a character from a horror movie. In fact, they can be quite helpful in managing the symptoms of bipolar disorder. Antipsychotics work by regulating the levels of dopamine in the brain, which can help control hallucinations, delusions, and other psychotic symptoms. Just be warned, they may come with some side effects. You might experience drowsiness, weight gain, or even a case of the infamous "restless leg syndrome." But don't worry; it's all part of the package deal.

And let's not forget about antidepressants. These little pills are designed to lift your spirits and combat those pesky depressive episodes. They work by increasing the levels of serotonin in the brain, which helps to improve mood and overall well-being. However, as with all good things in life, there can be some downsides. Antidepressants may cause sleep disturbances, weight gain, and, in rare cases, an increase in suicidal thoughts. But fear not; these side effects are closely monitored, and your healthcare provider will work with you to find the right balance.

Now, I know what you're thinking. "Do I really need all these medications? Can't I ride the rollercoaster of emotions and hope for the best?" Well, my friend, while that may sound like a thrilling adventure, it's not the most ideal approach. Bipolar disorder is a serious condition that requires proper management, and medication is an essential part of that. Think of it as your trusty sidekick, always by your side, helping you navigate the ups and downs of life.

But here's the thing: medication is not a one-size-fits-all solution. What works for one person may only work for one person. It's a bit like finding the perfect pair of jeans – it takes time and a lot of trial and error. So, don't be disheartened if the first medication you try doesn't quite hit the mark. Your healthcare provider will work with you to find the right combination and dosage that suits your unique needs.

Now, before we wrap up this chapter, let's address the elephant in the room – side effects. Yes, medications can have side effects, but remember, they are there to help you. It's all about weighing the pros and cons. Sure, you might experience some drowsiness or weight gain, but if it means living a more stable and fulfilling life, it's definitely worth it. And hey, you never know; those extra pounds might make you the life of the party!

Medication plays a vital role in managing bipolar disorder. From mood stabilizers to antipsychotics and antidepressants, these medications help keep your emotional rollercoaster in check. Yes, they may come with some side effects, but with the guidance of your healthcare provider, you can find the right balance. So, embrace your medication, embrace the stability, and get ready to thrive in the ups and downs of life with bipolar disorder. After all, you've got this, and your trusty sidekick is here to help you every step of the way.

Alternative and Complementary Therapies

Introducing acupuncture, Yoga, and mindfulness as complementary approaches to traditional treatment methods

In the world of bipolar disorder management, the quest for balance and stability can sometimes feel like a never-ending journey. While traditional treatment methods such as medication and therapy play a crucial role in managing the ups and downs, there is an emerging field that offers a unique and holistic approach to supplementing these interventions - alternative and complementary therapies.

Picture this: you're sitting in a room with tiny needles delicately placed on various parts of your body. No, it's not a scene from a horror movie; it's acupuncture, one of the alternative therapies that has gained traction in recent years. Acupuncture, rooted in traditional Chinese medicine, involves the insertion of thin needles into specific points along the body's energy pathways, known as meridians. This ancient practice aims to restore the flow of energy, or qi, promoting overall well-being and harmony within the body.

No, I know what you're thinking. Needles? No, thank you! But trust me, the benefits of acupuncture are worth overcoming any fear of pointy objects. Not only can it help alleviate symptoms of anxiety and depression, but studies have shown that acupuncture can also reduce the severity and frequency of bipolar mood swings. It's like hitting the bullseye with a needle!

Speaking of hitting the bullseye, let's move on to Yoga - the ancient practice that combines physical postures, breathing exercises, and meditation. When it comes to managing bipolar disorder, Yoga offers a myriad of benefits that can enhance traditional treatment methods. Not only does it improve flexibility and strength, but it also helps regulate mood, reduce stress, and promote a sense of inner calm. Plus, the added bonus of mastering those fancy yoga poses might earn you a spot on America's Got Talent!

Now, some of you might be thinking, "Yoga? I can't even touch my toes!" But fear not, my friends, because Yoga is for everyone. Whether you're a beginner or a seasoned yogi, there's a yoga practice out there that suits your needs. From gentle, restorative Yoga to more vigorous vinyasa flows, there's something for everyone on the yoga menu. And remember, it's not about touching your toes; it's about what you learn on the way down.

Last but certainly not least, let's dive into the realm of mindfulness. In a world that often feels chaotic and overwhelming, mindfulness offers a refuge of tranquility and self-awareness. This practice involves intentionally paying attention to the present moment without judgment or attachment. It's like hitting the pause button on the whirlwind of thoughts and emotions that accompany bipolar disorder.

So, how can mindfulness complement traditional treatment methods? Well, research has shown that practicing mindfulness can reduce stress, enhance emotional regulation, and improve overall well-being. By cultivating a non-judgmental awareness of our thoughts and feelings, we can better navigate the rollercoaster of bipolar disorder. It's like having a front-row seat to the circus of your mind without getting entangled in the acrobatics!

Now, I must warn you - engaging in these alternative and complementary therapies does not mean ditching your medication or therapy sessions. These approaches are valuable additions to your treatment plan, providing support and enhancing your overall well-being. As the saying goes, "Two heads are better than one," and the same goes for managing bipolar disorder. So why not embrace the power of acupuncture, Yoga, and mindfulness alongside traditional methods? It's like creating a symphony of interventions, where each instrument plays its unique part in achieving harmony and balance.

Remember, my fellow bipolar warriors, managing bipolar disorder is not a one-size-fits-all journey. It's a puzzle with many pieces, and alternative and complementary therapies are just a few of those pieces. So, grab your acupuncture needles, unroll your yoga mat, and embrace the present moment with open arms. Together, let's thrive in the ups and downs and discover the beauty of a holistic approach to managing bipolar disorder. And hey, if all else fails, at least we'll have some hilarious Yoga fails to share at our support group meetings! Namaste and laughter, my friends!

Chapter 4:
Navigating Relationships

Communication Strategies

Effective communication is a fundamental aspect of any successful relationship. Whether it be with your partner, family members, friends, or colleagues, the ability to communicate effectively fosters understanding, empathy, and, ultimately, stronger connections. In this chapter, we will explore various communication strategies that can help you navigate the ups and downs of relationships with bipolar disorder.

One key strategy to remember is active listening. It's not just about hearing the words being spoken but truly understanding and empathizing with the speaker. Practice giving your full attention, maintaining eye contact, and using non-verbal cues to show that you are engaged in the conversation. Remember, it's not about waiting for your turn to speak but genuinely listening and seeking to understand the other person's perspective.

Another essential technique is using "I" statements. When expressing your thoughts, feelings, or concerns, framing them in terms of how they impact you can help prevent defensiveness and encourage open dialogue. For example, instead of saying, "You always make me feel ignored," try saying, "I feel ignored when I don't get a chance to speak my mind." This small shift in language can make a significant difference in how your message is received.

Humor can also play a powerful role in communication. Using lighthearted jokes and anecdotes can help diffuse tension and create a more relaxed atmosphere. Of course, it's important to be mindful of the appropriateness and timing of your humor, but a well-placed joke can often break down barriers and make difficult conversations more manageable.

In addition to humor, employing metaphors and similes can be an effective way to clarify complex concepts or scenarios. Comparing a situation to something familiar can help bridge the gap in understanding between individuals with differing perspectives. For example, explaining the experience of bipolar disorder as a rollercoaster ride can help someone without the condition grasp the unpredictable ups and downs that individual with bipolar disorder face.

Non-verbal communication should not be overlooked either. Our body language, facial expressions, and tone of voice can convey just as much, if not more, than our words. Being aware of your non-verbal cues and actively using them to align with your verbal message can enhance understanding and build trust. For example, maintaining an open posture and a warm smile while expressing empathy can go a long way in fostering a deeper connection.

It's also important to recognize and address communication barriers that may arise in relationships affected by bipolar disorder. These barriers can include mood swings, impulsivity, and difficulty with concentration and memory. Being patient, understanding, and adapting your communication style to accommodate these challenges can make a significant difference in the quality of your interactions.

Ultimately, effective communication is a two-way street. It requires both parties to actively engage and make an effort to understand and be understood. By implementing these strategies, you can foster a more empathetic and understanding environment in your relationships, allowing for greater support and connection.

Remember, communication is a skill that can be learned and developed over time. It may take practice, patience, and the occasional misstep, but with dedication and a willingness to learn, you can enhance your communication abilities and cultivate healthier, more fulfilling relationships. So, let's start the journey of effective communication together - one conversation at a time, with a sprinkle of humor and a dash of empathy. After all, a little laughter and understanding can go a long way in navigating the ups and downs of bipolar disorder and thriving in relationships.

Intimacy and Sexuality
Addressing the Challenges and Strategies for Maintaining a Fulfilling Intimate Life while Managing Bipolar Disorder
When it comes to navigating the ups and downs of bipolar disorder, one aspect of life that can be particularly challenging is maintaining a fulfilling, intimate life. Bipolar disorder can impact many areas of a person's life, including their relationships and their sense of self. However, with the right strategies and a little creativity, it is possible to cultivate a satisfying and healthy intimate life while managing bipolar disorder.

One of the key challenges that individuals with bipolar disorder face when it comes to intimacy and sexuality is the impact of mood swings. During manic episodes, individuals may experience heightened sexual desire and engage in risky sexual behaviors. On the other hand, during depressive episodes, they may have a decreased interest in sex or struggle with feelings of low self-esteem and body image issues. These extreme fluctuations can make it difficult to establish and maintain a consistent and enjoyable intimate life.

So, how can one address these challenges and maintain a fulfilling, intimate life while managing bipolar disorder? It all starts with self-awareness and effective communication. Understanding your own mood patterns and triggers can help you anticipate and manage potential disruptions to your intimate life. By keeping a mood journal and tracking your emotions, you can gain valuable insights into how bipolar disorder affects your sexuality and intimacy.

Additionally, open and honest communication with your partner is vital. Let them know about the challenges you face and work together to develop strategies for maintaining intimacy during both manic and depressive episodes. This may involve setting boundaries, establishing a safe word or signal to indicate when you may need to pause or slow down, and exploring alternative ways of connecting physically and emotionally.

Another important aspect of maintaining a fulfilling, intimate life while managing bipolar disorder is prioritizing self-care. Taking care of your mental and physical health is crucial for overall well-being, and this extends to your intimate life as well. Engaging in regular Exercise, getting enough sleep, and managing stress can all contribute to a healthier and more satisfying intimate life.

It's also essential to have a support system in place. Surrounding yourself with understanding and empathetic friends and family members can make a world of difference. Not only can they provide emotional support, but they can also help you navigate the challenges that may arise in your intimate relationships.

Let's inject a little humor into this serious topic. Picture this: a support group specifically for individuals with bipolar disorder who are looking to spice up their intimate lives. We could call it "Bipolar Bliss" or "The Mood Swing Club." Imagine the laughter and camaraderie that would come from sharing experiences, tips, and even some hilarious mishaps. Who said living with bipolar disorder couldn't be entertaining?

In all seriousness, though, addressing the challenges of maintaining a fulfilling, intimate life while managing bipolar disorder requires a multifaceted approach. It involves self-awareness, effective communication, self-care, and a strong support system. By employing these strategies and maintaining a sense of humor along the way, individuals with bipolar disorder can cultivate a satisfying and healthy intimate life, one that embraces the unique challenges and triumphs of living with this condition.

So, don't let bipolar disorder hold you back from experiencing the joy and fulfillment of intimacy. Embrace the ups and downs, navigate the challenges with grace and humor, and remember that you are not alone on this journey. With the right strategies and a little laughter, a fulfilling, intimate life is within reach.

Parenting With Bipolar Disorder

Providing Guidance for Parents with Bipolar Disorder: Nurturing the Mind, Body, and Family Introduction: Parenting is a challenging journey, even without the added complexities of bipolar disorder. As a parent with bipolar disorder, you are not alone in facing unique obstacles and uncertainties. In this chapter, we will explore practical strategies and self-care tips that can help you manage your parenting responsibilities while nurturing your own mental health. By understanding and implementing these strategies, you can create a harmonious balance between your role as a parent and your journey with bipolar disorder.

Embracing Self-Care Parenthood often demands that we put our own needs on the back burner, but as someone with bipolar disorder, self-care becomes even more crucial. Here are some essential self-care tips to help you maintain stability. Prioritize Sleep: Make sleep a priority in your routine. Establish a consistent sleep schedule and create a calming bedtime routine. Consider using relaxation techniques such as meditation or listening to soothing music before sleep.2. Nourish Your Body: Maintain a balanced diet rich in nutrients that support mental well-being. Incorporate foods like salmon, walnuts, and leafy greens, which are known to boost mood and brain health. Remember to hydrate throughout the day and limit caffeine intake.3. Exercise for Your Mind and Body: Regular Exercise is a powerful tool for managing symptoms of bipolar disorder. Engage in activities that you enjoy, such as walking, Yoga, or dancing. Exercise releases endorphins, reduces stress, and improves overall mood.4. Practice Stress Management: Develop coping strategies to manage stress effectively. Consider techniques such as deep breathing exercises, journaling, or engaging in hobbies that bring you joy and relaxation. Find what works best for you and make it a part of your daily routine. Section 2: Effective Parenting Strategies Parenting with bipolar disorder requires careful planning and preparation. Here are some strategies to help you navigate the challenges and thrive as a parent. Create Consistency: Children thrive on routines, so establish consistent daily schedules that include regular mealtimes, bedtime routines, and designated family time. This structure helps both you and your child maintain stability and a sense of security.2. Open Communication: Create a safe space for open communication with your children. Please encourage them to express their feelings and concerns and be honest about your condition in an age-appropriate manner. Educate them about bipolar disorder, helping them understand your symptoms and how it may affect your family dynamics.3. Seek Support: Building a strong support network is crucial. Reach out to friends, family, or support groups who understand your journey with bipolar disorder. They can provide empathy, advice, and assistance when needed. Don't hesitate to ask for help when you need it.4. Teach Emotional Regulation: As someone with bipolar disorder, you have a unique understanding of the ups and downs of emotions. Please share your insights with your children and help them develop healthy coping mechanisms for managing their emotions. Encourage open conversations about feelings and model effective ways to regulate emotions. Section 3: Managing Parenting Responsibilities Balancing parenting responsibilities with bipolar disorder can be overwhelming. Here are some strategies to help you manage your daily tasks and minimize stress. Plan Ahead: Create daily and weekly schedules that include both parenting responsibilities and self-care activities. This proactive approach allows you to allocate time for both your children's needs and your own well-being. 2. Delegate and Accept Help: Don't be afraid to delegate tasks and accept help from others. Reach out to your partner, family members, or friends for support in managing household chores and child-rearing responsibilities. Remember, it takes a village to raise a child, and there is no shame in seeking assistance.3. Set Realistic Expectations: Recognize that you may have limitations due to your bipolar disorder. Set realistic expectations for yourself as a parent and accept that some days will be more challenging than others. Practice self-compassion and embrace the ups and downs of parenting with bipolar disorder. Parenting with bipolar disorder requires a delicate balance of self-care, effective parenting strategies, and support from your loved ones. By implementing the strategies discussed in this chapter, you can navigate the challenges with confidence and create a nurturing environment for both yourself and your children. Remember, you are not defined solely by your bipolar disorder but by the love and care you provide as a parent.

Embrace your unique journey and continue to thrive in the ups and downs of parenthood. After all, a little bit of chaos can make for an unforgettable adventure!

Disclosure and Workplace Support

Exploring the decision to disclose one's bipolar disorder in the workplace can feel like navigating a minefield. On the one hand, disclosing can lead to understanding and support from coworkers and employers. On the other hand, it can also lead to discrimination and prejudice. It's a delicate dance that many individuals with bipolar disorder face and one that requires careful consideration.

When it comes to disclosing your bipolar disorder, it's important to weigh the pros and cons. On the positive side, disclosing can open the door to workplace accommodations that can greatly enhance your ability to thrive in your job. These accommodations can range from flexible work hours to a modified workload, ensuring that you have the support you need to manage your symptoms effectively.

However, before making the decision to disclose, it's crucial to assess the workplace environment and the level of understanding and acceptance that exists. Unfortunately, not all workplaces are created equal when it comes to mental health awareness. Some may have stigmatizing attitudes and lack the necessary support systems in place. In such cases, disclosing may put you at risk of facing discrimination and even jeopardize your career.

To advocate for workplace accommodations, it's essential to educate both yourself and your employer about bipolar disorder. Take the time to research and gather information about the condition, its symptoms, and how it may impact your work. By arming yourself with knowledge, you can effectively communicate your needs and advocate for the necessary support.

When it comes to discussing your bipolar disorder with your employer, it can be helpful to have a plan in place. Prepare a list of accommodations that you believe would be beneficial for your specific situation. This could include options such as a quieter workspace, access to natural light, or the ability to take short breaks throughout the day. By presenting a well-thought-out plan, you are more likely to be taken seriously and have your needs addressed.

Of course, the decision to disclose is a personal one, and there is no one-size-fits-all approach. It's important to listen to your intuition and consider your own comfort level. If you feel that disclosing your bipolar disorder would be beneficial to your overall well-being and success in the workplace, then it may be worth taking the leap. Remember, you have the right to a supportive and accommodating work environment.

Now, let's lighten the mood with a little joke. Why did the bipolar employee bring a ladder to work? Because they wanted to reach new highs and avoid the lows of their workload! Jokes aside, navigating disclosure and workplace support can be challenging, but with the right approach and a supportive environment, individuals with bipolar disorder can thrive in their careers.

Chapter 5:
Coping with Triggers and Stress

Identifying Triggers

In the wild and unpredictable world of bipolar disorder, understanding what triggers your mood episodes is like having a secret weapon in your arsenal. It's like being able to predict the weather before anyone else, except instead of rain or sunshine, you're dealing with the stormy seas of mania and the dark depths of depression. But fear not, dear reader, for I am here to guide you through the treacherous waters of trigger identification and help you navigate your way to calmer shores.

So, what exactly are triggers? Triggers are those sneaky little devils that can send you spiraling into a mood episode faster than you can say, "I need a double shot of espresso." They can be external factors, like stress or a sudden change in routine, or internal factors, like lack of sleep or even certain foods. Triggers can be as unique and individual as a snowflake, which is why it's so important for you to become a master at identifying your own personal triggers.

Now, I know what you're thinking. "How on earth am I supposed to figure out what triggers my mood episodes when they seem to come out of nowhere like a pop-up thunderstorm?" Well, my friend, fear not. I have a few tricks up my sleeve that will help you on your quest for trigger identification.

First and foremost, keep a mood journal. I know, I know, it sounds about as exciting as watching paint dry, but trust me, it's worth it. Write down everything. How you're feeling, what you're doing, what you're eating, even the weather outside. You never know what seemingly insignificant detail might hold the key to unlocking the mystery of your triggers. Plus, it gives you an excuse to buy a fancy notebook and pretend you're a Victorian detective.

Next, pay attention to patterns. Are there certain situations or events that consistently precede a mood episode? Maybe it's that big work presentation that always sends you into a manic frenzy or the holidays that bring on a about of depression. Whatever it is, take note and start brainstorming ways to avoid or manage those triggers. Remember, knowledge is power, my friend.

And now, for my favorite part – the jokes. Why did the bipolar woman go to the bakery? Because she kneaded a little pick-me-up! Okay, maybe it's a little cheesy, but humor is a powerful tool in managing bipolar disorder. Laughter truly is the best medicine, so don't be afraid to find humor in your own ups and downs. After all, life is too short to be serious all the time.

Lastly, seek support. Whether it's through therapy, support groups, or even just a good old-fashioned vent session with a trusted friend, having someone to lean on can make all the difference in the world. They can help you identify triggers you may have missed, offer a different perspective, or be there to listen when you need to let it all out.

So, my fellow bipolar warriors, go forth and conquer the art of trigger identification. Arm yourself with your trusty mood journal, pay attention to patterns, and don't forget to laugh along the way. With a little bit of detective work and a whole lot of self-awareness, you'll soon be able to navigate the stormy seas of bipolar disorder with grace and resilience. You've got this.

Stress Management Techniques

Introducing various stress management techniques can be a game-changer when it comes to living well with bipolar disorder. After all, we all know that stress and bipolar disorder can be quite the tag team, wreaking havoc on our lives and sanity. So, it's time to arm ourselves with some effective stress-busting techniques that can help us thrive in the ups and downs of bipolar.

First up on our stress management arsenal is mindfulness. Ah, yes, the practice of being present at the moment and letting go of all those pesky worries and anxieties. Now, I know what you're thinking, "Really? Mindfulness? Isn't that just another fancy term for sitting around and doing nothing?" Well, my friend, let me tell you, mindfulness is anything but doing nothing. It's about taking control of your mind and focusing on the here and now. And trust me, when those racing thoughts are threatening to send you on a rollercoaster ride, mindfulness can be your saving grace.

Now, I won't lie to you. It takes some practice to master the art of mindfulness. But fear not, my fellow bipolar warriors, I've got a little trick up my sleeve to make it more fun. Picture this: you're sitting in your comfiest chair, eyes closed, and you're visualizing your thoughts as little fluffy clouds passing by. You can even give them funny names like "Mr. Worrisome" or "Ms. Anxiety Pants." As those clouds drift away, you'll find yourself feeling calmer and more at peace. And hey, who said stress management can't be entertaining?

Next on our stress-busting adventure is Exercise. Now, I know what you're thinking, "Exercise? But I already have enough on my plate with managing bipolar!" Trust me, I get it. The thought of hitting the gym or going for a run might seem daunting, especially when the lows of bipolar are dragging you down like an anchor. But here's the secret: Exercise doesn't have to be a grueling ordeal. Find something you love, whether it's dancing like nobody's watching, taking a leisurely stroll in nature, or even playing a game of ping pong. The key is to move your body and release those endorphins that can turn that frown upside down.

And let's remember the power of relaxation exercises. Picture this: you're lying in a warm bath, surrounded by aromatic candles, and listening to some soothing music. Ah, bliss! But relaxation exercises don't have to be limited to the bathroom. You can try deep breathing exercises, progressive muscle relaxation, or even indulge in a little bit of guided imagery. Whatever floats your boat and helps you unwind, my friend.

So, there you have it, my fellow bipolar warriors, a comprehensive guide to stress management techniques. Mindfulness, exercise, and relaxation exercises can be your secret weapons in the battle against stress. And remember, laughter is the best medicine, so remember to sprinkle a little humor into your stress-busting routine. After all, life is too short to be stressed all the time. So take a deep breath, find your happy place, and conquer stress like the bipolar champion that you are. You've got this!

Maintaining a Healthy Lifestyle

Promoting the Importance of Healthy Habits

In this segment of "Bipolar Women: Thriving in the Ups and Downs," we delve into the topic of maintaining a healthy lifestyle. We all know that taking care of our physical and mental well-being is essential, but sometimes life gets in the way, and we forget to prioritize our health. Well, fear not because we're here to remind you just how crucial it is to establish healthy habits, including regular sleep patterns, a balanced diet, and Exercise.

Let's start with sleep, shall we? Ah, sleep, that magical time when our bodies and minds recharge. Getting enough quality sleep is like hitting the reset button on our lives. It's the secret ingredient to feeling energized and ready to take on the world. So, how do we achieve this marvelous slumber? Well, first, you need to establish a regular sleep schedule. Try going to bed and waking up at the same time every day. Yes, even on weekends. I know it sounds like a cruel joke, but your body will thank you. And hey, if you struggle with falling asleep, I've got a trick up my sleeve. Are you counting sheep? Actually, that needs to be updated. Count your blessings instead. Trust me, it works like a charm.

Now, let's move on to the next piece of the puzzle: a balanced diet. Ah, food, the elixir of life. But not just any food will do. We need to fuel our bodies with the good stuff. So, what does a balanced diet look like? Well, it's all about variety, my friends. Think colorful fruits and vegetables, lean proteins, whole grains, and healthy fats. Oh, and remember the water. H2O is the nectar of the gods. It keeps us hydrated, our skin glowing, and our brains sharp. And let's remember the occasional treat.

Life is all about balance, after all. So, go ahead and indulge in that slice of chocolate cake. Just remember, moderation is key. And hey, did you hear about the new diet craze? It's called the "seafood diet." You see food, and you eat it. But seriously, folks, let's focus on nourishing our bodies and embracing the joy of good food.

Last but certainly not least, we come to exercise. Ah, Exercise, the ultimate mood booster. It's like a natural antidepressant, and the best part is that no prescription is needed. Moving our bodies not only keeps us physically fit but also releases those feel-good endorphins that make us feel on top of the world. Now, I know what you're thinking. Exercise is hard, and it requires effort. But trust me, once you find an activity you enjoy, it won't feel like a chore. Whether it's dancing, Yoga, hiking, or even chasing after your pet cat, find what gets you moving and stick with it. And if you need a little motivation, remember that Exercise is a great excuse to buy cute workout clothes. Who says you can't look fabulous while breaking a sweat?

So there you have it, folks. The trifecta of healthy habits: regular sleep patterns, a balanced diet, and Exercise. These three pillars will not only boost your physical and mental well-being but also set the foundation for a thriving life. Remember, taking care of yourself is not selfish; it's necessary. So go ahead, prioritize your health, and embrace the joy of a healthy lifestyle. And always remember, laughter is the best medicine. So, here's a joke to end on a high note: Why don't scientists trust atoms? Because they make up everything! Stay healthy, my friends!

Managing Work-Related Stress

In today's fast-paced and demanding work environment, it's no surprise that many of us experience work-related stress. Whether it's long hours, tight deadlines, or the constant pressure to perform, the stress can take a toll on our mental and physical well-being. But fear not! In this segment, we'll delve into strategies for handling work-related stress and maintaining a healthy work-life balance.

First and foremost, it's important to recognize the signs of work-related stress. Are you constantly feeling overwhelmed? Do you find it difficult to concentrate or make decisions? Are you experiencing physical symptoms like headaches or stomachaches? These are all red flags that indicate you may be dealing with excessive stress at work.

One effective strategy for managing work-related stress is to prioritize and organize your tasks. Create a to-do list and tackle the most important tasks first. Break larger projects into smaller, more manageable chunks. By focusing on one task at a time, you'll feel a sense of accomplishment and reduce the feeling of being overwhelmed.

Another valuable tool in combating work-related stress is learning to set boundaries. It's easy to let work consume our lives, but it's crucial to establish a healthy work-life balance. Set clear boundaries between work and personal life by creating designated times for relaxation and leisure activities. Remember, it's okay to say no to additional work or overtime if it infringes on your personal time.

In addition to setting boundaries, taking regular breaks throughout the workday is essential. Use your breaks to engage in activities that help you relax and recharge. Go for a walk, practice deep breathing exercises, or listen to your favorite music. These small moments of self-care can make a big difference in reducing stress levels.

Maintaining open communication with your colleagues and superiors is also key. If you're feeling overwhelmed or struggling with a particular task, don't hesitate to reach out for support. Asking for help is not a sign of weakness but rather a sign of strength and self-awareness. Remember, we're all in this together!

Finally, let's remember the importance of humor in managing work-related stress. Laughter truly is the best medicine, and injecting a bit of humor into your workday can do wonders for your stress levels. Share a funny anecdote with your coworkers, watch a comedic video during your lunch break, or keep a lighthearted, lighthearted joke on your desk to lift your spirits when things get tough.

So, my fellow warriors in the battle against work-related stress, remember to prioritize, set boundaries, take breaks, communicate openly, and never underestimate the power of a good laugh. With these strategies in your arsenal, you'll be well-equipped to conquer stress and maintain a healthy work-life balance. Stay strong, stay positive, and thrive in the face of adversity!

Coping With Life Transitions

Life is full of ups and downs, twists and turns, and unexpected detours. It's like being on a rollercoaster ride, but instead of simply enjoying the thrill, imagine trying to navigate those twists and turns while managing bipolar disorder. It can feel like you're strapped into that rollercoaster with no control over where it's going next. But fear not, my friends! In this segment of "Coping with Life Transitions," we're going to offer you some guidance on how to navigate those major life changes and transitions while keeping your bipolar disorder in check.

First and foremost, it's important to recognize that life transitions can be particularly challenging for those of us with bipolar disorder. Our mood swings can be triggered by even the smallest of changes, so when faced with major life events, it's like throwing a stick of dynamite into an already volatile volcano. But fret not, my fellow bipolar warriors, for we have a secret weapon – preparation.

When it comes to managing bipolar disorder during life transitions, preparation is key. Think of it as packing your metaphorical suitcase with all the tools and strategies you'll need to weather the storm. So grab your mental passport, and let's dive in!

One of the most important tools in your bipolar coping toolkit is self-care. It's like a magic potion that can help you navigate any storm that comes your way. So, during times of major life changes, make self-care your number one priority. Set aside time each day to do things that bring you joy and help you relax. Whether it's taking a bubble bath, going for a walk in nature, or indulging in a guilty pleasure (Netflix binge, anyone?), make sure you're taking care of yourself.

Another key strategy for managing bipolar disorder during life transitions is building a support system. Surround yourself with people who understand and support you. This could be friends, family, therapists, support groups – anyone who can offer a listening ear or a helping hand when you need it most. Remember, you don't have to face life's transitions alone. Reach out to your support system and let them be your rock.

Now, let's talk about the power of routine. Bipolar disorder loves routine, like I love a good cup of coffee in the morning – it's essential. During times of major life changes, try to establish a routine that provides structure and stability. This can help stabilize your mood and make the transition smoother. So, set a schedule for yourself and stick to it as much as possible. And hey, if life throws you a curveball and disrupts your routine, remember to be flexible and adapt. Life is full of surprises, after all.

Lastly, let's remember the importance of medication and therapy. During times of major life changes, it's crucial to stay on top of your treatment plan. Feel free to reach out to your healthcare provider if you're experiencing any changes in symptoms or if you need additional support. Remember, they're there to help you navigate these transitions and find the right balance for your bipolar disorder.

So, my friends, as we embark on this journey of coping with life transitions while managing bipolar disorder, remember that you are strong, resilient, and capable of weathering any storm that comes your way. With the right tools, strategies, and support, you can thrive in the ups and downs of life.

And hey, if all else fails, remember to laugh. Because sometimes, a good dose of laughter is the best medicine for navigating life's transitions. So, my fellow bipolar warriors, let's face those twists and turns with a smile on our faces and a hearty laugh in our hearts. After all, we've got this – bipolar and all.

Bipolar Women: Thriving in the Ups and Downs

Chapter 1

Understanding Bipolar Disorder

Explaining the Symptoms, Causes, and Diagnosis Picture this:

You're on a roller coaster, the wind whipping through your hair, the adrenaline coursing through your veins. You're soaring high, feeling invincible, and nothing can bring you down. But suddenly, the ride takes a sharp turn, hurtling you down into the depths of despair. Your heart races, your mind spins, and you can't catch your breath. This is what it's like to have bipolar disorder. Bipolar disorder, also known as manic-depressive illness, is a mental health condition that affects millions of people worldwide. It's like having two extreme personalities living inside you, constantly at odds with each other. One moment, you're on top of the world, bursting with energy and ideas. The next, you're plunged into a darkness so deep that it feels impossible to escape. So, what are the symptoms of bipolar disorder? Well, it's not as simple as just feeling happy one moment and sad the next. Bipolar disorder is characterized by distinct episodes of mania and depression. During a manic episode, you might feel euphoric, full of grandiose ideas, and have an almost superhuman level of energy. You might talk a mile a minute, take on multiple projects at once, and have difficulty sleeping. It's like your brain is running on overdrive, and there's no off switch. On the other hand, a depressive episode feels like being trapped in a deep, dark hole with no way out. You might feel hopeless, lethargic, and have a complete lack of interest in things that used to bring you joy. Simple tasks like getting out of bed or taking a shower become monumental challenges. It's like your world has been drained of color, and all you see is shades of gray. Now, you might be wondering, what causes bipolar disorder? Well, the exact cause is still unknown, but researchers believe it's a combination of genetic, biological, and environmental factors. It's like a perfect storm brewing inside your brain, waiting for the right trigger to set it off. It could be a stressful life event, a sudden change in routine, or even something as seemingly harmless as a change in sleep patterns. Diagnosing bipolar disorder can be a tricky business. After all, everyone has ups and downs, right? But when these ups and downs start interfering with your daily life, that's when it's time to seek help. A mental health professional will conduct a thorough evaluation, taking into account your symptoms, medical history, and family history. They might also ask you to keep a mood journal, tracking your emotions and behaviors over a period of time. Once diagnosed, it's important to remember that bipolar disorder is a chronic illness, but it's not a death sentence. With the right treatment plan, support system, and a dash of humor, you can learn to manage and thrive with bipolar disorder. It's like learning to ride that roller coaster with finesse, embracing the twists and turns, and finding joy in the ride. So, buckle up, my friend, because we're about to embark on a journey through the highs and lows of bipolar disorder. Together, we'll explore the intricacies of this condition, delve into the science behind it, and discover practical strategies for living well. And don't worry, I'll be right here with you, holding your hand and cracking a few jokes along the way. After all, laughter is the best medicine, right?

Prevalence in Women

When it comes to bipolar disorder, it's important to recognize that women and men can experience the condition differently. There are certain factors that make women more prone to bipolar disorder, and understanding these differences can help in effectively managing and living well with the condition. One of the key reasons why bipolar disorder affects women differently than men is the hormonal fluctuations that occur throughout their lives. Let's face it, ladies, our hormones can be like a rollercoaster ride at times – up, down, and all around! And unfortunately, these hormonal shifts can have a significant impact on our mental health. Take puberty, for example. As if dealing with acne and awkward growth spurts wasn't enough, our bodies are also experiencing a surge of hormones during this time. And research has shown that this hormonal imbalance can trigger the onset of bipolar disorder in some women. It's like getting a double whammy – not fair! But the hormonal challenges don't stop there, my friends. Oh no, we have to deal with the joys of menstruation too. Every month, like clockwork, our hormones go on a wild ride, wreaking havoc on our emotions and mental well-being. It's like having a permanent guest on the emotional rollercoaster, and it's no wonder that these fluctuations can exacerbate the symptoms of bipolar disorder. Pregnancy is another time when women are particularly vulnerable to the effects of bipolar disorder. The surge of hormones during pregnancy can cause a whirlwind of emotions and mood swings, which can be challenging to navigate for anyone, let alone someone with bipolar disorder. And let's not forget the postpartum period – the joy of welcoming a new bundle of joy is often accompanied by sleep deprivation, hormonal changes, and the infamous baby blues. For women with bipolar disorder, this can be a recipe for a serious mental health storm. Now, don't get me wrong, ladies. It's not all doom and gloom. We're strong, resilient beings, and we have the power to thrive despite these challenges. But it's essential to recognize and address the unique ways that bipolar disorder affects us. By understanding the prevalence of bipolar disorder in women and the factors that contribute to these differences, we can better manage our condition. It's about finding a balance, like walking a tightrope without falling off (and yes, I'm talking about both the hormonal tightrope and the mental health tightrope!). So, how can we do this? Well, education is key. Understanding our bodies, our hormones, and the ways in which they interact with bipolar disorder can empower us to make informed decisions about our mental health. We can work with healthcare professionals to develop personalized treatment plans that take into account our unique needs as women. Additionally, finding support is crucial. We are not alone in this journey, my friends. Connecting with others who have experienced similar challenges can provide a sense of camaraderie and understanding. And let's be real, having a tribe of badass bipolar women who can relate to your struggles and share a laugh (or a cry) with you is priceless. So, ladies, let's embrace our unique experiences with bipolar disorder. We may have to deal with hormonal rollercoasters and the occasional mood swing, but we are resilient. We are capable of thriving in the ups and downs. And with a little knowledge, support, and maybe a chocolate bar or two, we can navigate this journey with grace and humor. After all, laughter is the best medicine, right?

Impact on Relationships

Relationships can be a rollercoaster ride, even in the best of times. Throw bipolar disorder into the mix, and you've got a ride that could rival the wildest theme park attractions. Bipolar disorder has a way of impacting personal relationships, and if not managed properly, it can send those connections careening off the tracks. But fear not, my dear reader, for in this chapter, we will explore the impact of bipolar disorder on relationships and equip you with strategies to keep those connections thriving. When it comes to bipolar disorder, one of the most significant challenges lies in the unpredictable nature of the condition. The ups and downs, the highs and lows, can create a whirlwind of emotions that can be difficult for both the individual with bipolar disorder and their loved ones to navigate. One moment, you're basking in the glow of the person's infectious energy and zest for life, and the next, you find yourself caught in the eye of the storm, wondering where that person you know and love has gone. It's important to remember that bipolar disorder doesn't define a person's entire being. It's just one piece of the puzzle, albeit a significant one. Understanding this is crucial in maintaining healthy connections. Instead of solely focusing on the disorder, it's essential to see the person behind it – the person with hopes, dreams, and a beautiful soul. Communication is the key to any successful relationship, and this holds even more weight when bipolar disorder is involved. Open, honest, and compassionate communication can help bridge the gap between understanding and confusion. Encourage your loved one to express their feelings and concerns, and be prepared to do the same. And remember, my friend, a good laugh can go a long way. When discussing difficult topics, a well-timed joke can break the tension and remind you both that you're in this together, facing life's challenges side by side. Another strategy for maintaining healthy connections is to educate yourself about bipolar disorder. Arm yourself with knowledge, my friend, for knowledge is power. Learn about the symptoms, the triggers, and the treatment options. Understand that bipolar disorder is a complex condition, and it affects everyone differently. By educating yourself, you can better support your loved one and navigate the turbulent waters of their emotional landscape. Patience is a virtue, they say, and never has this been truer than when it comes to bipolar disorder and relationships. The highs and lows may come and go, but your love and support can remain steadfast. Remember that the person you care about is not their illness; they are a beautiful soul deserving of compassion and understanding. So, my friend, take a deep breath, count to ten if you must, and remind yourself that you're in this for the long haul. It's also essential to take care of yourself, for you cannot pour from an empty cup. Supporting someone with bipolar disorder can be emotionally taxing, and it's vital that you prioritize your own well-being. Set boundaries, seek support from friends and family, and engage in self-care activities that bring you joy and replenish your spirit. In conclusion, bipolar disorder can undoubtedly impact personal relationships, but it doesn't have to be the end of the world. With open communication, education, patience, and self-care, you can maintain healthy connections and thrive in the face of adversity. Remember, my dear reader, love knows no bounds, and together, you and your loved one can conquer the ups and downs of bipolar disorder, hand in hand, heart to heart. And if all else fails, well, a good laugh and a cheesy joke never hurt anyone. Why did the bipolar bear become a comedian? Because laughter is the best medicine, my friend, even for the wildest rollercoaster rides.

Stigma and Misconceptions

Addressing Common Misconceptions and Stigma Surrounding Bipolar Disorder in Women

In the realm of mental health, bipolar disorder is often misunderstood and stigmatized. This is especially true for women who are living with this condition. While the topic may seem daunting, it's important to address the common misconceptions and stigma surrounding bipolar disorder in women head-on. By doing so, we can foster understanding, support, and ultimately help women thrive in the ups and downs of their lives. So, let's dive into this often-misunderstood world and shed light on the truth behind the misconceptions.

Misconception 1: Women with bipolar disorder are unpredictable and dangerous.

Ah, the age-old stereotype of the "crazy woman." It's time to debunk this misconception once and for all. While it's true that bipolar disorder can lead to mood swings, it doesn't automatically make women dangerous or unpredictable. In fact, many women with bipolar disorder are incredibly self-aware and work diligently to manage their symptoms. So, the next time you encounter someone who says, "She's bipolar, so you never know what she'll do," kindly remind them that the majority of women with bipolar disorder are just like anyone else — kind, compassionate, and fully capable of leading fulfilling lives.

Misconception 2: Women with bipolar disorder are incapable of maintaining healthy relationships.

This misconception couldn't be further from the truth. Yes, bipolar disorder presents unique challenges when it comes to relationships, but with proper management and support, women with bipolar disorder can maintain healthy and fulfilling connections. It's all about communication, understanding, and a little bit of patience. So, the next time you hear someone say, "I could never date someone with bipolar disorder," gently remind them that love and understanding can conquer any obstacle, including mental health conditions.

Misconception 3: Women with bipolar disorder are always in a manic or depressive state.

Contrary to popular belief, bipolar disorder doesn't mean a constant rollercoaster ride of extreme emotions. In reality, there are periods of stability and balance for individuals with bipolar disorder. This misconception often stems from media portrayals that sensationalize the extremes, neglecting to show the everyday experiences of those living with bipolar disorder. So, the next time someone says, "She must be in a manic phase," educate them about the complexities of bipolar disorder and how it can manifest differently in each individual.

Misconception 4: Women with bipolar disorder cannot lead successful and fulfilling lives.

Ah, the misconception that breaks our hearts. Women with bipolar disorder are capable of achieving incredible success and finding fulfillment in their lives. It's important to remember that mental health conditions do not define a person's worth or potential. By sharing stories of resilience, creativity, and accomplishment, we can inspire others and break down the barriers of stigma. So, the next time you encounter someone who believes that women with bipolar disorder are destined for a life of struggle, share stories of women who have defied the odds and are thriving in their personal and professional lives.

Addressing Stigma:

Now that we've addressed some of the common misconceptions surrounding bipolar disorder in women, let's talk about the stigma that often accompanies this condition. Stigma can manifest in various ways, from discriminatory attitudes to social exclusion. It's crucial to address and combat this stigma to create a more inclusive and understanding society.

Education is key. By increasing awareness and providing accurate information about bipolar disorder, we can dispel myths and misconceptions. Let's encourage open conversations about mental health, where individuals feel safe to share their experiences without fear of judgment.

Support networks are vital. Women living with bipolar disorder often benefit from connecting with others who can relate to their experiences. Support groups, online communities, and therapy can provide a sense of belonging and validation. Together, we can create a supportive environment where women with bipolar disorder feel empowered to seek help and support.

Challenging language and stereotypes. Words have power, and the language we use can perpetuate stigma or challenge it. Let's move away from derogatory labels and instead focus on compassionate and inclusive language when discussing mental health conditions. By doing so, we create a safe space for individuals to seek help and feel understood.

In conclusion, addressing the common misconceptions and stigma surrounding bipolar disorder in women is a crucial step towards creating a more compassionate and supportive society. By promoting understanding, empathy, and accurate information, we can empower women with bipolar disorder to thrive in their lives, embracing both the ups and downs with resilience and strength. So, let's challenge the misconceptions, break down the barriers, and pave the way for a world where every woman can live well with bipolar disorder. Remember, together, we can make a difference – one stigma at a time.

And now, to lighten the mood, here's a little joke for you: Why did the bipolar woman bring a ladder to the bar? She was ready for the highs and lows of the night! Remember, laughter is often the best medicine, even when addressing serious topics.

Seeking Professional Help

Seeking Professional Help: Guiding You to the Right Healthcare Providers and the Importance of a Comprehensive Treatment Plan

In the journey of managing bipolar disorder, seeking professional help is like finding the perfect pair of shoes - it may take some time and a few blisters, but once you find the right fit, it can make all the difference. In this chapter, we will explore the importance of finding the right healthcare providers and the value of a comprehensive treatment plan. So, grab your metaphorical magnifying glass and let's embark on this investigative journey together!

When it comes to finding healthcare providers, it's crucial to remember that you are the detective in charge of your own mental health case. It's easy to feel overwhelmed by the sheer number of psychiatrists, therapists, and other professionals out there. But fear not, dear reader, for I have a few tricks up my sleeve to help you navigate this maze.

First and foremost, it's essential to find professionals who specialize in bipolar disorder. Think of it this way: you wouldn't go to a dentist for a broken bone, would you? Well, the same logic applies here. Seek out experts who have extensive knowledge and experience in treating bipolar disorder.

They'll know the ins and outs of the condition, the latest treatment options, and can tailor their approach to suit your unique needs.

Now, you may be wondering, "But how do I find these unicorn-like professionals?" Fear not, for I shall guide you through the wilderness of online directories and recommendations. Start by asking for referrals from your primary care physician, friends, or support groups. Word-of-mouth recommendations can be like gold in the realm of mental healthcare. If that doesn't yield any leads, turn to trusted online resources that specialize in mental health provider directories. These directories often include detailed profiles, reviews, and ratings to help you make an informed decision.

Once you've gathered a list of potential providers, it's time to put your detective skills to the test. Schedule an initial consultation with each of them, treating it like a detective's interrogation (minus the trench coat and fedora). Come prepared with a list of questions that delve into their expertise, treatment approach, and what they had for breakfast (okay, maybe not the last one). This meeting is your chance to assess their compatibility with your needs, gauge their communication style, and see if they have a sense of humor that matches your own. After all, laughter can be the best medicine, especially when life throws you a bipolar-shaped curveball.

Now, let's shift gears and talk about the importance of a comprehensive treatment plan. Picture it as a roadmap guiding you through the winding roads of bipolar disorder. Just as you wouldn't embark on a cross-country road trip without a GPS, you shouldn't navigate your mental health journey without a well-crafted plan.

A comprehensive treatment plan involves a multi-pronged approach that encompasses medication, therapy, self-care, and support systems. It's like assembling a superhero team, with each member playing a vital role in your well-being. Medication acts as the powerful shield, reducing the intensity of mood swings. Therapy becomes the wise sage, helping you uncover the root causes of your struggles and equipping you with coping strategies. Self-care serves as the trusty sidekick, reminding you to prioritize your mental and physical health. And your support system? Well, they're the Avengers, standing by your side when things get tough.

Remember, dear reader, that a comprehensive treatment plan is not a one-size-fits-all solution. It's an evolving masterpiece, crafted specifically for you and your unique journey. Adjustments will be made, detours may be taken, but with each step, you'll be inching closer to a life of stability and fulfillment.

Now, I know what you're thinking – "This all sounds great, but how do I stay motivated when the going gets tough?" Ah, my dear reader, let me share a secret weapon with you - the power of humor. Laughter has the incredible ability to ease tension, brighten even the darkest of days, and remind us that we're not alone in this bipolar rollercoaster ride. So, don't be afraid to sprinkle some humor into your treatment plan. Whether it's finding joy in the little things, cracking jokes with your therapist, or indulging in a good old-fashioned comedy show, humor can be a powerful tool in your arsenal.

In conclusion, dear reader, seeking professional help is a critical step in your bipolar journey. By finding the right healthcare providers and crafting a comprehensive treatment plan, you'll be equipping yourself with the tools and support needed to thrive in the ups and downs of bipolar disorder. So, put on your detective hat, embrace your sense of humor, and let the journey towards mental wellness begin!

Remember, my dear reader, you're the hero of this story. And with the right support and a dash of humor, you'll conquer every twist and turn that bipolar disorder throws your way. Stay strong, stay resilient, and most importantly, stay hopeful. The road may be bumpy, but you have everything you need to thrive in the ups and downs of life with bipolar disorder. Keep seeking help, keep crafting that comprehensive treatment plan, and always remember - you are not alone.

Chapter 2:
Understanding Bipolar Disorder

Different Types of Bipolar Disorder

When it comes to bipolar disorder, it's not a one-size-fits-all kind of situation. Oh no, my friends, there are different types of this wild ride called bipolar disorder, each with their own unique characteristics. It's like going to a theme park and trying out all the different roller coasters – except these roller coasters are happening inside your brain. Fun, right? Well, maybe not always, but we're here to explore these various subtypes and shed some light on what makes them special.

First up, we have good old bipolar I disorder. This is the granddaddy of them all, the one that gets all the attention. It's like the front row seat on the roller coaster – you get to experience the highest highs and the lowest lows. With bipolar I, you might find yourself soaring to the heights of mania, feeling like you can conquer the world. But watch out, because those manic episodes can quickly turn into a downward spiral of depression. It's a wild ride, my friends, but at least you'll never be bored.

Next, we have bipolar II disorder. Think of this as the roller coaster in the middle – not as intense as the front row, but still enough to get your heart racing. With bipolar II, you'll experience hypomania, which is like a watered-down version of full-blown mania. It's like having a shot of espresso without the sugar rush. You'll feel energized, creative, and maybe a little impulsive. But don't worry, because after the hypomania comes the crash into depression. It's like the post-coffee crash, but on a whole other level.

Now, let's talk about cyclothymic disorder. This one's like the kiddie coaster at the theme park – it's not as extreme, but it still has its ups and downs. With cyclothymic disorder, you'll experience milder versions of mania and depression, but they'll still be enough to make you feel like you're on a wild ride. It's like the teacup ride that spins you around and around – you'll feel dizzy and disoriented, but at least it's not as intense as the big roller coasters.

And finally, we have rapid-cycling bipolar disorder. This one's like being on a roller coaster that never stops. With rapid-cycling, you'll experience four or more episodes of mania, hypomania, or depression within a year. It's like being on the world's longest roller coaster – you're constantly going up and down, up and down. It can be exhausting, but hey, at least you'll never have a dull moment.

So, there you have it, folks – the different types of bipolar disorder. Each one has its own unique characteristics, its own ups and downs. It's like having a whole theme park inside your brain. But remember, just like at a theme park, there are ways to manage and enjoy the ride. Medication, therapy, and a solid support system can make all the difference. And hey, a sense of humor doesn't hurt either. So, buckle up, my friends, and get ready for the ride of your life. It may be a wild one, but with the right tools and a dash of laughter, you can thrive in the ups and downs of bipolar disorder.

Symptoms and Warning Signs

In the tumultuous sea of emotions that is bipolar disorder, women often find themselves navigating treacherous waves that threaten to engulf them. But fear not, dear reader, for in this segment, we shall explore the common symptoms and warning signs of bipolar disorder in women. So grab your life vest and let's dive in!

The Ups and Downs of Bipolar Disorder:

Picture this: you're riding the roller coaster of life, but instead of being confined to the tracks, you find yourself hurtling through the clouds one moment, and plunging into the depths of despair the next. Welcome to the world of bipolar disorder. This mental health condition is characterized by extreme mood swings, ranging from the highs of mania to the lows of depression. And women, oh how they can dance between these extremes with a finesse that would make even the most seasoned tightrope walker envious.

The Manic Marvels:

Ah, the exhilaration of a manic episode! It's like strapping yourself to a rocket ship and blasting off into a universe where sleep is optional and ideas flow faster than a river in spring. During these manic episodes, women with bipolar disorder may exhibit a range of symptoms, such as heightened energy levels, racing thoughts, an inflated sense of self-importance, and a penchant for taking on multiple projects at once. It's like having a thousand tabs open in your brain, except you're the one who opened them all!

The Depressive Depths:

But what goes up must come down, and when it comes to bipolar disorder, the descent into depression can be a harrowing experience. Women with bipolar disorder may find themselves trapped in a fog of sadness, hopelessness, and an overwhelming fatigue that makes even the simplest tasks feel like climbing Mount Everest. It's like being stuck in a never-ending rainstorm, with no umbrella in sight.

The Mixed Bag:

Just when you thought you had bipolar disorder all figured out, it throws you a curveball in the form of a mixed episode. Imagine feeling the energy of mania coursing through your veins, but with the darkness of depression weighing you down like a lead balloon. Women experiencing a mixed episode may find themselves restless, agitated, and prone to impulsive behavior. It's like trying to dance the tango while wearing roller skates - a thrilling yet precarious balancing act.

The Red Flags:

Now that we've explored the wild terrain of bipolar disorder, let's shine a spotlight on the warning signs that may signal its presence. Women with bipolar disorder may experience changes in sleep patterns, appetite, and concentration. They may also exhibit irritability, racing thoughts, and a loss of interest in activities they once enjoyed. It's like having a neon sign flashing "Something's not quite right!" in the back of your mind.

Seeking Help and Support:

Remember, dear reader, you are not alone in this journey. There are lifelines available to help you navigate the turbulent waters of bipolar disorder. Seeking professional help from a mental health expert is essential, as they can provide a diagnosis, develop a treatment plan, and offer invaluable support. Additionally, reaching out to friends, family, and support groups can provide a lifeline of understanding and empathy. Together, we can weather the storm and emerge stronger than ever before.

In the symphony of life, bipolar disorder adds an unexpected melody that can be both beautiful and challenging. By highlighting the common symptoms and warning signs of bipolar disorder in women, we hope to shed light on this often-misunderstood condition. So, dear reader, may you embrace your ups and downs with grace, finding strength in your journey and thriving in the face of adversity. And remember, when life hands your lemons, make a deliciously tart lemonade, spiked with resilience and a splash of humor. Cheers to thriving in the ups and downs of bipolar disorder!

Triggers and Risk Factors

In order to truly understand and manage bipolar disorder, it is crucial to identify the triggers and risk factors that can contribute to its onset and exacerbation. These factors can vary from person to person, but they often fall into three main categories: environmental, genetic, and lifestyle. Let's take a closer look at each of these factors, shall we?

Firstly, let's talk about the environmental triggers. These are the external factors that can potentially disrupt the delicate balance of the brain and lead to the manifestation of bipolar symptoms. Stress, for instance, is a notorious trigger that can send our moods spiraling in either direction. Whether it's work-related stress, relationship troubles, or even just the demands of daily life, stress has a knack for pushing our emotional buttons. But fear not! Remember, stress is like a blender without a lid - it may splatter everywhere, but with a little mindfulness, you can keep it contained.

Next up, we have the genetic factors. Bipolar disorder has a strong genetic component, meaning that if you have a family member with the condition, your risk of developing it is significantly higher. Now, I know what you're thinking - "Great, I won the genetic lottery!" But fear not, my friend, because genetics are only part of the equation. It's like having a loaded gun; it doesn't necessarily mean you'll pull the trigger. Understanding your genetic predisposition can actually be empowering. It allows you to be proactive in managing your mental health and implementing strategies to prevent triggers from taking control.

Last but not least, we have lifestyle factors. These are the choices we make in our day-to-day lives that can either fuel the fire or douse the flames of bipolar disorder. Sleep, for instance, plays a pivotal role in maintaining stability. Without enough sleep, our mood can resemble a rollercoaster ride on steroids. So, make sure to prioritize those Zzz's and create a bedtime routine that would make even the Sandman proud. And speaking of routines, having a consistent daily schedule can work wonders in managing bipolar symptoms. It's like having a roadmap for your day, ensuring you stay on track and avoid any detours into emotional turbulence.

Now, before we move on, let's take a moment to appreciate the absurdity of life. I mean, who would have thought that a disorder with such a serious impact on our lives would have triggers that sound like the ingredients for a wacky sitcom? Stress, genetics, and sleep—it's like the start of a bad joke. But here's the punchline: by understanding and addressing these triggers, we can take back control and thrive in the face of bipolar disorder.

So, my fellow bipolar warriors, take a deep breath, embrace your uniqueness, and remember that life is a comedy, not a tragedy. By identifying and managing these triggers and risk factors, you are equipped with the tools to live well and thrive in the ups and downs of bipolar disorder. And hey, if all else fails, just remember that laughter truly is the best medicine. So go ahead, find the humor in life's quirks, and let your spirit soar. After all, a little laughter can go a long way in keeping those moods in check. Keep on thriving, my friends!

Comorbidities and Dual Diagnosis

Examining the Connection Between Bipolar Disorder and Other Mental Health Conditions

Picture this: You're sitting in a crowded waiting room, nervously fidgeting with your appointment reminder. The clock on the wall seems to be moving at a snail's pace, as if time itself is playing a cruel joke on you. Finally, the door opens, and you are called in to meet your psychiatrist. As you enter the room, you can't help but notice the stacks of medical textbooks piled high on the shelves, each one seemingly thicker than the last. You take a deep breath and prepare yourself for what lies ahead—the daunting task of unraveling the complex web of comorbidities and dual diagnosis.

Comorbidities, as the name suggests, refer to the presence of two or more medical conditions occurring simultaneously in an individual. In the realm of mental health, comorbidities can be like unexpected guests crashing a party. Just when you thought you had bipolar disorder to contend with, in walks anxiety, depression, or substance abuse. It's as if life decided to throw a curveball your way, just to keep things interesting. But fear not! Understanding the connection between bipolar disorder and these comorbid conditions can shed light on the path to managing and living well with this challenging disorder.

Let's start with anxiety. If bipolar disorder was a rollercoaster ride, anxiety would be the tightrope you walk while on it. The constant worry, the racing thoughts, the gnawing feeling in the pit of your stomach—these are all familiar companions to those with bipolar disorder. It's like having a battle royale between your mind and body, each one vying for dominance. But here's the twist: anxiety can actually be a symptom of bipolar disorder itself, or it can be a separate condition that just happens to tag along for the ride. Either way, it's important to address anxiety head-on, because let's face it, nobody wants to be on the edge of their seat all the time—unless they're at a thrilling movie or a stand-up comedy show.

Moving on to depression, it's like the rainy days that follow a thunderstorm. Bipolar disorder already takes you on a wild ride, swinging from the highs of mania to the lows of depression. But when depression decides to cozy up and make itself at home, it's like adding insult to injury. You may find yourself feeling down, hopeless, and lacking the energy to even get out of bed in the morning. But fear not, my friend, for there is hope! Understanding the interplay between bipolar disorder and depression can help you navigate through the stormy seas and find the silver lining in even the darkest of clouds.

Now, let's address the elephant in the room — substance abuse. It's like a mischievous imp that sneaks its way into your life, wreaking havoc along the way. Bipolar disorder and substance abuse often go hand in hand, like the proverbial peanut butter and jelly. Many individuals with bipolar disorder turn to drugs or alcohol as a way to self-medicate, to numb the pain, or to escape the relentless rollercoaster of emotions. But here's the catch: substance abuse not only exacerbates the symptoms of bipolar disorder, but it can also interfere with the effectiveness of medications and treatment. It's like pouring gasoline on a fire, hoping it will put it out — it's just not going to work. So, my friend, put down that shot glass or that pack of cigarettes, and let's embark on a journey towards a healthier, happier you.

The connection between bipolar disorder and other mental health conditions is like a tangled web that requires careful unraveling. By understanding the intricacies of comorbidities and dual diagnosis, you can better equip yourself with the tools to manage and live well with bipolar disorder. Remember, you are not alone in this journey. Seek support, whether it be from mental health professionals, support groups, or trusted friends and family. And above all, never lose sight of the fact that you have the strength and resilience to thrive in the ups and downs of life. So, my friend, hold on tight — it's going to be one heck of a ride!

And hey, remember that old saying: "Laugh in the face of adversity." So, here's a little joke to lighten the mood:

Why did the bipolar bear go to therapy?

Because he was tired of feeling bipolar — he wanted to be a pro-polar!

Okay, okay, I know it's a cheesy joke, but hey, laughter is the best medicine, right? So, my friend, keep smiling, keep learning, and keep thriving. You've got this!

Managing Mood Episodes

Living with bipolar disorder can often feel like a rollercoaster ride, with its ups and downs, twists and turns. One moment, you may find yourself soaring high with energy, creativity, and confidence, while the next, you may plummet into a deep and dark abyss of depression and despair. These extreme mood swings, known as manic and depressive episodes, can be incredibly challenging to navigate. But fear not, for in this chapter, we will explore practical strategies for managing these mood episodes and finding stability amidst the chaos.

Let's start with manic episodes. Picture this: you're feeling on top of the world, like you could conquer anything and everything. You have a million ideas racing through your mind, and you just can't seem to slow down. While it may be tempting to embrace this surge of energy and productivity, it's crucial to maintain a balance. One strategy is to channel your manic energy into productive outlets, such as creative projects or physical activities. Paint a masterpiece, write a novel, or run a marathon — the possibilities are endless! Just remember to pace yourself and avoid overexertion, as it can lead to burnout.

Now, let's switch gears and talk about depressive episodes. Imagine waking up one morning and feeling like you're carrying the weight of the world on your shoulders. Everything feels hopeless, and even the simplest tasks seem insurmountable. In these moments, it's important to practice self-care and reach out for support. Surround yourself with a strong support network of friends, family, and mental health professionals who can offer a listening ear and a helping hand. Engage in activities that bring you joy, whether it's cuddling up with a good book, going for a walk in nature, or indulging in some retail therapy (within reason, of course!).

Another strategy for managing both manic and depressive episodes is to establish a routine. Bipolar disorder often disrupts our natural circadian rhythms, leading to erratic sleep patterns and irregular daily routines. By setting a consistent schedule for sleep, meals, exercise, and medication, you can provide a sense of stability and structure in your life. It may take some trial and error to find a routine that works for you, but once you do, stick to it like glue — well, maybe not as sticky as glue, but you get the point!

In addition to routine, it's crucial to prioritize self-awareness and self-monitoring. Learn to recognize the early warning signs of both manic and depressive episodes. Are you sleeping less, talking faster, and engaging in impulsive behaviors? These may be indicators of an impending manic episode. On the other hand, if you find yourself sleeping excessively, feeling fatigued, and withdrawing from activities you once enjoyed, it may be a sign of depression creeping in. By being attuned to these warning signs, you can take proactive measures to manage your mood episodes before they spiral out of control.

Of course, managing mood episodes is not a one-size-fits-all approach. Each person's experience with bipolar disorder is unique, and what works for one may not work for another. It's important to consult with a mental health professional who can tailor a treatment plan specifically for you. Medication, therapy, and lifestyle adjustments can all play a role in managing your mood episodes effectively. Remember, you are not alone in this journey, and with the right support and strategies, you can thrive in the ups and downs of bipolar disorder.

Now, before we wrap up this chapter, let me leave you with a little joke to lighten the mood. Why did the bipolar bear bring a ladder to the party? Because he wanted to reach new heights — both literally and metaphorically! Okay, maybe that was a bit cheesy, but humor has its way of bringing a smile to our faces even in the darkest of times.

So, dear reader, as you continue on your path of managing mood episodes, remember to be kind to yourself, stay resilient, and embrace the journey of living well with bipolar disorder. You are capable, you are strong, and you have the power to thrive in the ups and downs.

Chapter 3:
Building a Support System

Family and Friends

Advising on How to Educate Loved Ones about Bipolar Disorder and Involve Them in the Recovery Process

As we navigate the ups and downs of bipolar disorder, one thing becomes abundantly clear - we can't do it alone. Our family and friends play a crucial role in our journey towards managing and thriving with this condition. However, sometimes, they might not fully understand what bipolar disorder entails or how they can support us effectively. That's why it's essential to educate our loved ones about bipolar disorder and involve them in our recovery process. So, grab a cup of coffee, gather your family and friends around, and let's dive into some practical advice on how to make this happen.

First and foremost, it's essential to approach the topic with empathy, patience, and a touch of humor. Bipolar disorder can be a heavy subject, but sprinkling in some jokes can help lighten the mood and make it more approachable. For example, you could say something like, "Did you know that living with bipolar disorder is like riding a rollercoaster? Except, instead of cotton candy and a souvenir photo, you get mood swings and a medication schedule."

Now that you have their attention, it's time to educate them about bipolar disorder. Start by explaining the basics - what it is and how it affects you. Use simple, concrete language that they can easily understand. Imagine you're explaining it to a child, but without sounding condescending. Remember, the goal is to provide them with a solid foundation of knowledge, so they can better grasp what you're going through.

To help them understand the highs and lows of bipolar disorder, you can use metaphors and similes. For instance, you might say, "During a manic episode, it's like my brain becomes a racecar on a never-ending track, zooming from one thought to another at lightning speed. But during a depressive episode, it's like my brain turns into a cozy blanket fort on a rainy day, where it's hard to find the motivation to do anything."

Once they have a grasp of the basics, it's time to involve them in your recovery process. Explain the importance of support networks and how their presence and understanding can make a world of difference. Encourage them to ask questions and express their concerns openly. This open line of communication will help foster a sense of trust and enable them to provide the support you need.

Additionally, consider inviting them to therapy sessions or support group meetings. This can be an eye-opening experience for them, as they witness firsthand the challenges you face and the strategies you employ to manage your condition. It also allows them to connect with others who may be going through similar experiences, further strengthening their understanding and empathy.

It's important to remember that educating loved ones about bipolar disorder is an ongoing process. Be patient with them and yourself, as it might take time for them to fully grasp the complexities of the condition. Encourage them to continue learning and seeking out resources that can enhance their understanding.

In conclusion, involving our family and friends in our journey with bipolar disorder is vital for our overall well-being. By educating them about the condition and inviting them to be part of our recovery process, we create a support network that can make all the difference. So, next time you gather your loved ones around, armed with coffee and a few well-placed jokes, remember that you're not just informing them about bipolar disorder – you're inviting them to be an essential part of your thriving and thriving together.

Support Groups and Therapy

Support groups and therapy are two powerful tools that can greatly benefit individuals living with bipolar disorder. While it may be tempting to brush off these resources as unnecessary or ineffective, the truth is that they can play a pivotal role in managing and thriving with this condition. In this chapter, we will delve into the benefits of participating in support groups and therapy, shedding light on why they are so essential for individuals with bipolar disorder.

Let's start with support groups. Imagine a room filled with people who truly understand what you're going through – the highs, the lows, and everything in between. That's the beauty of support groups. These gatherings provide a safe and non-judgmental space for individuals with bipolar disorder to connect with others who share similar experiences. It's like having a tribe of people who just "get it."

Support groups offer a multitude of benefits. Firstly, they help combat feelings of isolation and loneliness that often accompany bipolar disorder. When you're surrounded by a supportive community, you no longer feel like you're navigating this journey alone. You have people who can empathize with your struggles and offer genuine understanding and encouragement.

Additionally, support groups provide a platform for sharing coping strategies and tips for managing bipolar symptoms. Each person brings their unique perspective and experiences to the table, creating a rich pool of knowledge and wisdom. From practical advice on medication management to innovative self-care techniques, these groups become a treasure trove of information.

But it's not just about receiving support; it's also about giving it. By actively participating in support groups, individuals with bipolar disorder can offer their own insights and support to others. This act of helping and supporting others can be incredibly empowering and fulfilling, boosting self-esteem and fostering a sense of purpose.

Now, let's turn our attention to therapy. Therapy, whether it's individual or group-based, can be a game-changer for individuals with bipolar disorder. The therapeutic setting provides a safe and confidential space to explore thoughts, emotions, and behaviors, with the guidance of a trained professional.

Therapy helps individuals with bipolar disorder develop essential coping skills and strategies to manage their symptoms effectively. Through various therapeutic techniques, such as cognitive-behavioral therapy (CBT) or dialectical behavior therapy (DBT), individuals learn to identify triggers, regulate their emotions, and develop healthy coping mechanisms.

One of the significant benefits of therapy is the opportunity to gain a deeper understanding of oneself and one's condition. By working closely with a therapist, individuals can uncover patterns and triggers that contribute to their bipolar symptoms. This newfound insight allows them to make informed choices and take proactive steps towards better mental health.

Therapy also provides a space for individuals to explore and address any underlying emotional or psychological issues that may be exacerbating their bipolar disorder. Sometimes, unresolved trauma or unresolved grief can significantly impact one's mental well-being. Therapy offers a safe container to process these emotions and work towards healing.

Now, you might be thinking, "But therapy is so serious! Is there any room for humor?" Absolutely! Humor can be a powerful tool in therapy, helping individuals lighten the mood and find some levity amidst the challenges they face. In fact, some therapists even use humor intentionally to create a more relaxed and comfortable atmosphere.

Imagine this scenario: you're sitting in therapy, discussing the ups and downs of bipolar disorder, when suddenly, your therapist cracks a well-timed joke. It catches you off guard, and you find yourself bursting into laughter. In that moment, the weight of your struggles feels a little lighter, and you realize that even in the darkest times, there can be moments of joy and laughter.

In conclusion, support groups and therapy offer invaluable benefits for individuals with bipolar disorder. They provide a sense of community, a wealth of knowledge, and a safe space to heal and grow. So, if you're living with bipolar disorder, don't hesitate to explore these resources. Embrace the power of connection and therapy, and take the first step towards living well with bipolar disorder. Remember, you don't have to face this journey alone. Together, we can thrive in the ups and downs of bipolar disorder!

Self-Care and Lifestyle Changes

Promoting self-care practices and lifestyle adjustments that can enhance overall well-being is an essential aspect of managing bipolar disorder. In this chapter, we will explore various strategies and techniques that can help individuals with bipolar disorder thrive in their daily lives.

Self-care is not a luxury; it is a necessity for individuals with bipolar disorder. It involves taking deliberate actions to improve one's physical, emotional, and mental well-being. One of the most crucial aspects of self-care is establishing a consistent daily routine. This routine should include regular sleep patterns, exercise, and healthy eating habits.

Sleep is particularly vital for individuals with bipolar disorder, as disruptions in sleep can trigger mood swings. It's essential to prioritize getting enough sleep and maintaining a consistent sleep schedule. Avoiding caffeine and electronic devices before bedtime can also help promote better sleep.

Exercise is another important self-care practice that can have a significant impact on mood stability. Engaging in regular physical activity, whether it's going for a walk, practicing yoga, or participating in a favorite sport, can help release endorphins, reduce stress, and improve overall well-being. Remember, exercise doesn't have to be intense or time-consuming; even short bursts of activity can make a difference.

Eating a balanced and nutritious diet is also crucial for individuals with bipolar disorder. Certain foods, such as those rich in omega-3 fatty acids, can help reduce inflammation in the brain and improve mood. Incorporating foods like fatty fish, walnuts, and flaxseeds into your diet can provide these essential nutrients. Additionally, limiting the consumption of processed foods, sugar, and alcohol can help stabilize mood and improve overall health.

In addition to these self-care practices, there are lifestyle adjustments that can enhance well-being for individuals with bipolar disorder. One such adjustment is the practice of stress management techniques. Stress can exacerbate symptoms of bipolar disorder, so finding healthy ways to manage and reduce stress is crucial. This could include activities such as meditation, deep breathing exercises, journaling, or engaging in hobbies that bring joy and relaxation.

Another lifestyle adjustment that can greatly impact overall well-being is the establishment of a strong support system. Surrounding oneself with understanding and supportive friends, family, or support groups can provide a sense of belonging and help individuals navigate the challenges of bipolar disorder. Being able to openly communicate about one's experiences and emotions can be incredibly empowering.

It's important to note that self-care and lifestyle adjustments are not a one-size-fits-all solution. Each individual with bipolar disorder is unique, and it may take some trial and error to find the strategies and practices that work best for you. Be patient with yourself and allow room for experimentation.

Promoting self-care practices and making lifestyle adjustments are essential components of managing bipolar disorder. By prioritizing sleep, exercise, nutrition, stress management, and building a strong support system, individuals with bipolar disorder can enhance their overall well-being and thrive in their daily lives. So, embrace self-care, make those lifestyle changes, and let your inner light shine through the ups and downs of bipolar disorder!

The Role of Medication

One of the key components in managing bipolar disorder is medication. It plays a crucial role in stabilizing mood swings and reducing the intensity of manic and depressive episodes. But what exactly are these medications and how do they work? Let's dive into the world of bipolar medication and explore the different types and potential side effects.

First up, we have mood stabilizers. These medications, as the name suggests, help to stabilize and regulate mood fluctuations. Lithium, for example, is a commonly prescribed mood stabilizer that has been used for decades. It's like the superhero of medications, swooping in to save the day and keep those manic and depressive episodes at bay. However, like any superhero, it does have some side effects. It can cause tremors, weight gain, and even impact your thyroid function. But hey, it's a small price to pay for emotional stability, right?

Next on the list are antipsychotics. Now, don't let the name scare you. These medications are not about to turn you into a character from a horror movie. In fact, they can be quite helpful in managing the symptoms of bipolar disorder. Antipsychotics work by regulating the levels of dopamine in the brain, which can help control hallucinations, delusions, and other psychotic symptoms. Just be warned, they may come with some side effects. You might experience drowsiness, weight gain, or even a case of the infamous "restless leg syndrome." But don't worry, it's all part of the package deal.

And let's not forget about antidepressants. These little pills are designed to lift your spirits and combat those pesky depressive episodes. They work by increasing the levels of serotonin in the brain, which helps to improve mood and overall well-being. However, as with all good things in life, there can be some downsides. Antidepressants may cause sleep disturbances, weight gain, and, in rare cases, an increase in suicidal thoughts. But fear not, these side effects are closely monitored, and your healthcare provider will work with you to find the right balance.

Now, I know what you're thinking. "Do I really need all these medications? Can't I just ride the rollercoaster of emotions and hope for the best?" Well, my friend, while that may sound like a thrilling adventure, it's not the most ideal approach. Bipolar disorder is a serious condition that requires proper management, and medication is an essential part of that. Think of it as your trusty sidekick, always by your side, helping you navigate the ups and downs of life.

But here's the thing, medication is not a one-size-fits-all solution. What works for one person may not work for another. It's a bit like finding the perfect pair of jeans — it takes time and a lot of trial and error. So, don't be disheartened if the first medication you try doesn't quite hit the mark. Your healthcare provider will work with you to find the right combination and dosage that suits your unique needs.

Now, before we wrap up this chapter, let's address the elephant in the room — side effects. Yes, medications can have side effects, but remember, they are there to help you. It's all about weighing the pros and cons. Sure, you might experience some drowsiness or weight gain, but if it means living a more stable and fulfilling life, it's definitely worth it. And hey, you never know, those extra pounds might just make you the life of the party!

Medication plays a vital role in managing bipolar disorder. From mood stabilizers to antipsychotics and antidepressants, these medications help keep your emotional rollercoaster in check. Yes, they may come with some side effects, but with the guidance of your healthcare provider, you can find the right balance. So, embrace your medication, embrace the stability, and get ready to thrive in the ups and downs of life with bipolar disorder. After all, you've got this, and your trusty sidekick is here to help you every step of the way.

Alternative and Complementary Therapies

Introducing acupuncture, yoga, and mindfulness as complementary approaches to traditional treatment methods

In the world of bipolar disorder management, the quest for balance and stability can sometimes feel like a never-ending journey. While traditional treatment methods such as medication and therapy play a crucial role in managing the ups and downs, there is an emerging field that offers a unique and holistic approach to supplementing these interventions - alternative and complementary therapies.

Picture this: you're sitting in a room with tiny needles delicately placed on various parts of your body. No, it's not a scene from a horror movie; it's acupuncture, one of the alternative therapies that has gained traction in recent years. Acupuncture, rooted in traditional Chinese medicine, involves the insertion of thin needles into specific points along the body's energy pathways, known as meridians. This ancient practice aims to restore the flow of energy, or qi, promoting overall well-being and harmony within the body.

No, I know what you're thinking. Needles? No thank you! But trust me, the benefits of acupuncture are worth overcoming any fear of pointy objects. Not only can it help alleviate symptoms of anxiety and depression, but studies have shown that acupuncture can also reduce the severity and frequency of bipolar mood swings. It's like hitting the bullseye with a needle!

Speaking of hitting the bullseye, let's move on to yoga - the ancient practice that combines physical postures, breathing exercises, and meditation. When it comes to managing bipolar disorder, yoga offers a myriad of benefits that can enhance traditional treatment methods. Not only does it improve flexibility and strength, but it also helps regulate mood, reduce stress, and promote a sense of inner calm. Plus, the added bonus of mastering those fancy yoga poses might just earn you a spot on America's Got Talent!

Now, I understand that some of you might be thinking, "Yoga? I can't even touch my toes!" But fear not, my friends, because yoga is for everyone. Whether you're a beginner or a seasoned yogi, there's a yoga practice out there that suits your needs. From gentle, restorative yoga to more vigorous vinyasa flows, there's something for everyone on the yoga menu. And remember, it's not about touching your toes; it's about what you learn on the way down.

Last but certainly not least, let's dive into the realm of mindfulness. In a world that often feels chaotic and overwhelming, mindfulness offers a refuge of tranquility and self-awareness. This practice involves intentionally paying attention to the present moment, without judgment or attachment. It's like hitting the pause button on the whirlwind of thoughts and emotions that accompany bipolar disorder.

So how can mindfulness complement traditional treatment methods? Well, research has shown that practicing mindfulness can reduce stress, enhance emotional regulation, and improve overall well-being. By cultivating a nonjudgmental awareness of our thoughts and feelings, we can better navigate the rollercoaster of bipolar disorder. It's like having a front-row seat to the circus of your mind, without getting entangled in the acrobatics!

Now, I must warn you – engaging in these alternative and complementary therapies does not mean ditching your medication or therapy sessions. These approaches should be seen as valuable additions to your treatment plan, providing support and enhancing your overall well-being. As the saying goes, "two heads are better than one," and the same goes for managing bipolar disorder. So why not embrace the power of acupuncture, yoga, and mindfulness alongside traditional methods? It's like creating a symphony of interventions, where each instrument plays its unique part in achieving harmony and balance.

Remember, my fellow bipolar warriors, managing bipolar disorder is not a one-size-fits-all journey. It's a puzzle with many pieces, and alternative and complementary therapies are just a few of those pieces. So, grab your acupuncture needles, unroll your yoga mat, and embrace the present moment with open arms. Together, let's thrive in the ups and downs, and discover the beauty of a holistic approach to managing bipolar disorder. And hey, if all else fails, at least we'll have some hilarious yoga fails to share at our support group meetings! Namaste and laughter, my friends!

Chapter 4:
Navigating Relationships

Communication Strategies

Effective communication is a fundamental aspect of any successful relationship. Whether it be with your partner, family members, friends, or colleagues, the ability to communicate effectively fosters understanding, empathy, and ultimately, stronger connections. In this chapter, we will explore various communication strategies that can help you navigate the ups and downs of relationships with bipolar disorder.

One key strategy to remember is active listening. It's not just about hearing the words being spoken, but truly understanding and empathizing with the speaker. Practice giving your full attention, maintaining eye contact, and using non-verbal cues to show that you are engaged in the conversation. Remember, it's not about waiting for your turn to speak, but genuinely listening and seeking to understand the other person's perspective.

Another essential technique is using "I" statements. When expressing your thoughts, feelings, or concerns, framing them in terms of how they impact you can help prevent defensiveness and encourage open dialogue. For example, instead of saying, "You always make me feel ignored," try saying, "I feel ignored when I don't get a chance to speak my mind." This small shift in language can make a significant difference in how your message is received.

Humor can also play a powerful role in communication. Using light-hearted jokes and anecdotes can help diffuse tension and create a more relaxed atmosphere. Of course, it's important to be mindful of the appropriateness and timing of your humor, but a well-placed joke can often break down barriers and make difficult conversations more manageable.

In addition to humor, employing metaphors and similes can be an effective way to clarify complex concepts or scenarios. Comparing a situation to something familiar can help bridge the gap in understanding between individuals with differing perspectives. For example, explaining the experience of bipolar disorder as a rollercoaster ride can help someone without the condition grasp the unpredictable ups and downs that individual with bipolar disorder face.

Non-verbal communication should not be overlooked either. Our body language, facial expressions, and tone of voice can convey just as much, if not more, than our words. Being aware of your non-verbal cues and actively using them to align with your verbal message can enhance understanding and build trust. For example, maintaining an open posture and a warm smile while expressing empathy can go a long way in fostering a deeper connection.

It's also important to recognize and address communication barriers that may arise in relationships affected by bipolar disorder. These barriers can include mood swings, impulsivity, and difficulty with concentration and memory. Being patient, understanding, and adapting your communication style to accommodate these challenges can make a significant difference in the quality of your interactions.

Ultimately, effective communication is a two-way street. It requires both parties to actively engage and make an effort to understand and be understood. By implementing these strategies, you can foster a more empathetic and understanding environment in your relationships, allowing for greater support and connection.

Remember, communication is a skill that can be learned and developed over time. It may take practice, patience, and the occasional misstep, but with dedication and a willingness to learn, you can enhance your communication abilities and cultivate healthier, more fulfilling relationships. So, let's start the journey of effective communication together - one conversation at a time, with a sprinkle of humor and a dash of empathy. After all, a little laughter and understanding can go a long way in navigating the ups and downs of bipolar disorder and thriving in relationships.

Intimacy and Sexuality

Addressing the Challenges and Strategies for Maintaining a Fulfilling Intimate Life while Managing Bipolar Disorder

When it comes to navigating the ups and downs of bipolar disorder, one aspect of life that can be particularly challenging is maintaining a fulfilling intimate life. Bipolar disorder can impact many areas of a person's life, including their relationships and their sense of self. However, with the right strategies and a little creativity, it is possible to cultivate a satisfying and healthy intimate life while managing bipolar disorder.

One of the key challenges that individuals with bipolar disorder face when it comes to intimacy and sexuality is the impact of mood swings. During manic episodes, individuals may experience heightened sexual desire and engage in risky sexual behaviors. On the other hand, during depressive episodes, they may have a decreased interest in sex or struggle with feelings of low self-esteem and body image issues. These extreme fluctuations can make it difficult to establish and maintain a consistent and enjoyable intimate life

So, how can one address these challenges and maintain a fulfilling intimate life while managing bipolar disorder? It all starts with self-awareness and effective communication. Understanding your own mood patterns and triggers can help you anticipate and manage potential disruptions to your intimate life. By keeping a mood journal and tracking your emotions, you can gain valuable insights into how bipolar disorder affects your sexuality and intimacy.

Additionally, open and honest communication with your partner is vital. Let them know about the challenges you face and work together to develop strategies for maintaining intimacy during both manic and depressive episodes. This may involve setting boundaries, establishing a safe word or signal to indicate when you may need to pause or slow down, and exploring alternative ways of connecting physically and emotionally.

Another important aspect of maintaining a fulfilling intimate life while managing bipolar disorder is prioritizing self-care. Taking care of your mental and physical health is crucial for overall well-being, and this extends to your intimate life as well. Engaging in regular exercise, getting enough sleep, and managing stress can all contribute to a healthier and more satisfying intimate life.

It's also essential to have a support system in place. Surrounding yourself with understanding and empathetic friends and family members can make a world of difference. Not only can they provide emotional support, but they can also help you navigate the challenges that may arise in your intimate relationships.

Now, let's inject a little humor into this serious topic, shall we? Picture this: a support group specifically for individuals with bipolar disorder who are looking to spice up their intimate lives. We could call it "Bipolar Bliss" or "The Mood Swing Club." Imagine the laughter and camaraderie that would come from sharing experiences, tips, and even some hilarious mishaps. Who said living with bipolar disorder couldn't be entertaining?

In all seriousness, though, addressing the challenges of maintaining a fulfilling intimate life while managing bipolar disorder requires a multifaceted approach. It involves self-awareness, effective communication, self-care, and a strong support system. By employing these strategies and maintaining a sense of humor along the way, individuals with bipolar disorder can cultivate a satisfying and healthy intimate life, one that embraces the unique challenges and triumphs of living with this condition.

So, don't let bipolar disorder hold you back from experiencing the joy and fulfillment of intimacy. Embrace the ups and downs, navigate the challenges with grace and humor, and remember that you are not alone on this journey. With the right strategies and a little laughter, a fulfilling intimate life is within reach.

Parenting With Bipolar Disorder

Providing Guidance for Parents with Bipolar Disorder: Nurturing the Mind, Body, and Family Introduction: Parenting is a challenging journey, even without the added complexities of bipolar disorder. As a parent with bipolar disorder, you are not alone in facing unique obstacles and uncertainties. In this chapter, we will explore practical strategies and self-care tips that can help you manage your parenting responsibilities while nurturing your own mental health. By understanding and implementing these strategies, you can create a harmonious balance between your role as a parent and your journey with bipolar disorder.

Embracing Self-Care Parenthood often demands that we put our own needs on the backburner, but as someone with bipolar disorder, self-care becomes even more crucial. Here are some essential self-care tips to help you maintain stability:1. Prioritize Sleep: Make sleep a priority in your routine. Establish a consistent sleep schedule and create a calming bedtime routine. Consider using relaxation techniques such as meditation or listening to soothing music before sleep.2. Nourish Your Body: Maintain a balanced diet rich in nutrients that support mental well-being. Incorporate foods like salmon, walnuts, and leafy greens, which are known to boost mood and brain health. Remember to hydrate throughout the day and limit caffeine intake.3. Exercise for Your Mind and Body: Regular exercise is a powerful tool for managing bipolar disorder symptoms. Engage in activities that you enjoy, such as walking, yoga, or dancing. Exercise releases endorphins, reduces stress, and improves overall mood.4. Practice Stress Management: Develop coping strategies to effectively manage stress. Consider techniques such as deep breathing exercises, journaling, or engaging in hobbies that bring you joy and relaxation. Find what works best for you and make it a part of your daily routine. Section 2: Effective Parenting Strategies Parenting with bipolar disorder requires careful planning and preparation. Here are some strategies to help you navigate the challenges and thrive as a parent:1. Create Consistency: Children thrive on routines, so establish consistent daily schedules that include regular mealtimes, bedtime routines, and designated family time. This structure helps both you and your child maintain stability and a sense of security.2. Open Communication: Create a safe space for open communication with your children. Encourage them to express their feelings and concerns, and be honest about your condition in an age-appropriate manner. Educate them about bipolar disorder, helping them understand your symptoms and how it may affect your family dynamics.3. Seek Support: Building a strong support network is crucial. Reach out to friends, family, or support groups who understand your journey with bipolar disorder. They can provide empathy, advice, and assistance when needed. Don't hesitate to ask for help when you need it.4. Teach Emotional Regulation: As someone with bipolar disorder, you have a unique understanding of the ups and downs of emotions. Share your insights with your children and help them develop healthy coping mechanisms for managing their emotions. Encourage open conversations about feelings and model effective ways to regulate emotions. Section 3: Managing Parenting Responsibilities Balancing parenting responsibilities with bipolar disorder can be overwhelming. Here are some strategies to help you manage your daily tasks and minimize stress:1. Plan Ahead: Create daily and weekly schedules that include both parenting responsibilities and self-care activities. This proactive approach allows you to allocate time for both your children's needs and your own well-being.2. Delegate and Accept Help: Don't be afraid to delegate tasks and accept help from others. Reach out to your partner, family members, or friends for support in managing household chores and child-rearing responsibilities. Remember, it takes a village to raise a child, and there is no shame in seeking assistance.3. Set Realistic Expectations: Recognize that you may have limitations due to your bipolar disorder. Set realistic expectations for yourself as a parent and accept that some days will be more challenging than others. Practice self-compassion and embrace the ups and downs of parenting with bipolar disorder. Parenting with bipolar disorder requires a delicate balance of self-care, effective parenting strategies, and support from your loved ones. By implementing the strategies discussed in this chapter, you can navigate the challenges with confidence and create a nurturing environment for both yourself and your children. Remember, you are not defined solely by your bipolar disorder but by the love and care you provide as a parent. Embrace your unique journey and continue to thrive in the ups and downs of parenthood. After all, a little bit of chaos can make for an unforgettable adventure!

Disclosure and Workplace Support

Exploring the decision to disclose one's bipolar disorder in the workplace can feel like navigating a minefield. On one hand, disclosing can lead to understanding and support from coworkers and employers. On the other hand, it can also lead to discrimination and prejudice. It's a delicate dance that many individuals with bipolar disorder face, and one that requires careful consideration.

When it comes to disclosing your bipolar disorder, it's important to weigh the pros and cons. On the positive side, disclosing can open the door to workplace accommodations that can greatly enhance your ability to thrive in your job. These accommodations can range from flexible work hours to a modified workload, ensuring that you have the support you need to manage your symptoms effectively.

However, before making the decision to disclose, it's crucial to assess the workplace environment and the level of understanding and acceptance that exists. Unfortunately, not all workplaces are created equal when it comes to mental health awareness. Some may have stigmatizing attitudes and lack the necessary support systems in place. In such cases, disclosing may put you at risk of facing discrimination and even jeopardize your career.

To advocate for workplace accommodations, it's essential to educate both yourself and your employer about bipolar disorder. Take the time to research and gather information about the condition, its symptoms, and how it may impact your work. By arming yourself with knowledge, you can effectively communicate your needs and advocate for the necessary support.

When it comes to discussing your bipolar disorder with your employer, it can be helpful to have a plan in place. Prepare a list of accommodations that you believe would be beneficial for your specific situation. This could include options such as a quieter workspace, access to natural light, or the ability to take short breaks throughout the day. By presenting a well-thought-out plan, you are more likely to be taken seriously and have your needs addressed.

Of course, the decision to disclose is a personal one, and there is no one-size-fits-all approach. It's important to listen to your intuition and consider your own comfort level. If you feel that disclosing your bipolar disorder would be beneficial to your overall well-being and success in the workplace, then it may be worth taking the leap. Remember, you have the right to a supportive and accommodating work environment.

Now, let's lighten the mood with a little joke. Why did the bipolar employee bring a ladder to work? Because they wanted to reach new highs and avoid the lows of their workload! Jokes aside, navigating disclosure and workplace support can be challenging, but with the right approach and a supportive environment, individuals with bipolar disorder can thrive in their careers.

Chapter 5:
Coping with Triggers and Stress

Identifying Triggers

In the wild and unpredictable world of bipolar disorder, understanding what triggers your mood episodes is like having a secret weapon in your arsenal. It's like being able to predict the weather before anyone else, except instead of rain or sunshine, you're dealing with the stormy seas of mania and the dark depths of depression. But fear not, dear reader, for I am here to guide you through the treacherous waters of trigger identification and help you navigate your way to calmer shores.

So, what exactly are triggers? Triggers are those sneaky little devils that can send you spiraling into a mood episode faster than you can say "I need a double shot of espresso." They can be external factors, like stress or a sudden change in routine, or internal factors, like lack of sleep or even certain foods. Triggers can be as unique and individual as a snowflake, which is why it's so important for you to become a master at identifying your own personal triggers.

Now, I know what you're thinking. "How on earth am I supposed to figure out what triggers my mood episodes when they seem to come out of nowhere like a pop-up thunderstorm?" Well, my friend, fear not. I have a few tricks up my sleeve that will help you on your quest for trigger identification.

First and foremost, keep a mood journal. I know, I know, it sounds about as exciting as watching paint dry, but trust me, it's worth it. Write down everything. How you're feeling, what you're doing, what you're eating, even the weather outside. You never know what seemingly insignificant detail might hold the key to unlocking the mystery of your triggers. Plus, it gives you an excuse to buy a fancy notebook and pretend you're a Victorian detective.

Next, pay attention to patterns. Are there certain situations or events that consistently precede a mood episode? Maybe it's that big work presentation that always sends you into a manic frenzy or the holidays that bring on a bout of depression. Whatever it is, take note and start brainstorming ways to avoid or manage those triggers. Remember, knowledge is power, my friend.

And now, for my favorite part—the jokes. Why did the bipolar woman go to the bakery? Because she kneaded a little pick-me-up! Okay, maybe it's a little cheesy, but humor is a powerful tool in managing bipolar disorder. Laughter truly is the best medicine, so don't be afraid to find the humor in your own ups and downs. After all, life is too short to be serious all the time.

Lastly, seek support. Whether it's through therapy, support groups, or even just a good old-fashioned vent session with a trusted friend, having someone to lean on can make all the difference in the world. They can help you identify triggers you may have missed, offer a different perspective, or simply be there to listen when you need to let it all out.

So, my fellow bipolar warriors, go forth and conquer the art of trigger identification. Arm yourself with your trusty mood journal, pay attention to patterns, and don't forget to laugh along the way. With a little bit of detective work and a whole lot of self-awareness, you'll soon be able to navigate the stormy seas of bipolar disorder with grace and resilience. You've got this.

Stress Management Techniques

Introducing various stress management techniques can be a game-changer when it comes to living well with bipolar disorder. After all, we all know that stress and bipolar disorder can be quite the tag team, wreaking havoc on our lives and sanity. So, it's time to arm ourselves with some effective stress-busting techniques that can help us thrive in the ups and downs of bipolar.

First up on our stress management arsenal is mindfulness. Ah, yes, the practice of being present in the moment and letting go of all those pesky worries and anxieties. Now, I know what you're thinking, "Really? Mindfulness? Isn't that just another fancy term for sitting around and doing nothing?" Well, my friend, let me tell you, mindfulness is anything but doing nothing. It's about taking control of your mind and focusing on the here and now. And trust me, when those racing thoughts are threatening to send you on a rollercoaster ride, mindfulness can be your saving grace.

Now, I won't lie to you. It takes some practice to master the art of mindfulness. But fear not, my fellow bipolar warriors, I've got a little trick up my sleeve to make it more fun. Picture this: you're sitting in your comfiest chair, eyes closed, and you're visualizing your thoughts as little fluffy clouds passing by. You can even give them funny names like "Mr. Worrisome" or "Ms. Anxiety Pants." As those clouds drift away, you'll find yourself feeling calmer and more at peace. And hey, who said stress management can't be entertaining?

Next on our stress-busting adventure is exercise. Now, I know what you're thinking, "Exercise? But I already have enough on my plate with managing bipolar!" Trust me, I get it. The thought of hitting the gym or going for a run might seem daunting, especially when the lows of bipolar are dragging you down like an anchor. But here's the secret: exercise doesn't have to be a grueling ordeal. Find something you love, whether it's dancing like nobody's watching, taking a leisurely stroll in nature, or even playing a game of ping pong. The key is to move your body and release those endorphins that can turn that frown upside down.

And let's not forget about the power of relaxation exercises. Picture this: you're lying in a warm bath, surrounded by aromatic candles, and listening to some soothing music. Ah, bliss! But relaxation exercises don't have to be limited to the bathroom. You can try deep breathing exercises, progressive muscle relaxation, or even indulge in a little bit of guided imagery. Whatever floats your boat and helps you unwind, my friend.

So, there you have it, my fellow bipolar warriors, a comprehensive guide to stress management techniques. Mindfulness, exercise, and relaxation exercises can be your secret weapons in the battle against stress. And remember, laughter is the best medicine, so don't forget to sprinkle a little humor into your stress-busting routine. After all, life is too short to be stressed all the time. So take a deep breath, find your happy place, and conquer stress like the bipolar champion that you are. You've got this!

Maintaining a Healthy Lifestyle

Promoting the Importance of Healthy Habits

In this segment of "Bipolar Women: Thriving in the Ups and Downs," we delve into the topic of maintaining a healthy lifestyle. We all know that taking care of our physical and mental well-being is essential, but sometimes life gets in the way and we forget to prioritize our health. Well, fear not, because we're here to remind you just how crucial it is to establish healthy habits, including regular sleep patterns, a balanced diet, and exercise.

Let's start with sleep, shall we? Ah, sleep, that magical time when our bodies and minds recharge. Getting enough quality sleep is like hitting the reset button on our lives. It's the secret ingredient to feeling energized and ready to take on the world. So, how do we achieve this marvelous slumber? Well, first, you need to establish a regular sleep schedule. Try going to bed and waking up at the same time every day. Yes, even on weekends. I know, it sounds like a cruel joke, but your body will thank you. And hey, if you struggle with falling asleep, I've got a trick up my sleeve. Counting sheep? No, that's outdated. Count your blessings instead. Trust me, it works like a charm.

Now, let's move on to the next piece of the puzzle: a balanced diet. Ah, food, the elixir of life. But not just any food will do. We need to fuel our bodies with the good stuff. So, what does a balanced diet look like? Well, it's all about variety, my friends. Think colorful fruits and vegetables, lean proteins, whole grains, and healthy fats. Oh, and don't forget the water. H2O is the nectar of the gods. It keeps us hydrated, our skin glowing, and our brains sharp. And let's not forget about the occasional treat. Life is all about balance, after all. So, go ahead, indulge in that slice of chocolate cake. Just remember, moderation is key. And hey, did you hear about the new diet craze? It's called the "seafood diet." You see food, and you eat it. But seriously, folks, let's focus on nourishing our bodies and embracing the joy of good food.

Last but certainly not least, we come to exercise. Ah, exercise, the ultimate mood booster. It's like a natural antidepressant, and the best part is, no prescription needed. Moving our bodies not only keeps us physically fit but also releases those feel-good endorphins that make us feel on top of the world. Now, I know what you're thinking. Exercise is hard, and it requires effort. But trust me, once you find an activity you enjoy, it won't feel like a chore. Whether it's dancing, yoga, hiking, or even chasing after your pet cat, find what gets you moving and stick with it. And if you need a little motivation, just remember that exercise is a great excuse to buy cute workout clothes. Who says you can't look fabulous while breaking a sweat?

So there you have it, folks. The trifecta of healthy habits: regular sleep patterns, a balanced diet, and exercise. These three pillars will not only boost your physical and mental well-being but also set the foundation for a thriving life. Remember, taking care of yourself is not selfish; it's necessary. So go ahead, prioritize your health, and embrace the joy of a healthy lifestyle. And always remember, laughter is the best medicine. So, here's a joke to end on a high note: Why don't scientists trust atoms? Because they make up everything! Stay healthy, my friends!

Managing Work-Related Stress

In today's fast-paced and demanding work environment, it's no surprise that many of us experience work-related stress. Whether it's long hours, tight deadlines, or the constant pressure to perform, the stress can take a toll on our mental and physical well being. But fear not! In this segment, we'll delve into strategies for handling work-related stress and maintaining a healthy work-life balance.

First and foremost, it's important to recognize the signs of work-related stress. Are you constantly feeling overwhelmed? Do you find it difficult to concentrate or make decisions? Are you experiencing physical symptoms like headaches or stomachaches? These are all red flags that indicate you may be dealing with excessive stress at work.

One effective strategy for managing work-related stress is to prioritize and organize your tasks. Create a to-do list and tackle the most important tasks first. Break larger projects into smaller, more manageable chunks. By focusing on one task at a time, you'll feel a sense of accomplishment and reduce the feeling of being overwhelmed.

Another valuable tool in combating work-related stress is learning to set boundaries. It's easy to let work consume our lives, but it's crucial to establish a healthy work-life balance. Set clear boundaries between work and personal life by creating designated times for relaxation and leisure activities. Remember, it's okay to say no to additional work or overtime if it infringes on your personal time.

In addition to setting boundaries, taking regular breaks throughout the workday is essential. Use your breaks to engage in activities that help you relax and recharge. Go for a walk, practice deep breathing exercises, or listen to your favorite music. These small moments of self-care can make a big difference in reducing stress levels.

Maintaining open communication with your colleagues and superiors is also key. If you're feeling overwhelmed or struggling with a particular task, don't hesitate to reach out for support. Asking for help is not a sign of weakness, but rather a sign of strength and self-awareness. Remember, we're all in this together!

Finally, let's not forget the importance of humor in managing work-related stress. Laughter truly is the best medicine, and injecting a bit of humor into your workday can do wonders for your stress levels. Share a funny anecdote with your coworkers, watch a comedic video during your lunch break, or keep a lighthearted joke on your desk to lift your spirits when things get tough.

So, my fellow warriors in the battle against work-related stress, remember to prioritize, set boundaries, take breaks, communicate openly, and never underestimate the power of a good laugh. With these strategies in your arsenal, you'll be well-equipped to conquer stress and maintain a healthy work-life balance. Stay strong, stay positive, and thrive in the face of adversity!

Coping With Life Transitions

Life is full of ups and downs, twists and turns, and unexpected detours. It's like being on a rollercoaster ride, but instead of simply enjoying the thrill, imagine trying to navigate those twists and turns while managing bipolar disorder. It can feel like you're strapped into that rollercoaster with no control over where it's going next. But fear not, my friends! In this segment of "Coping with Life Transitions," we're going to offer you some guidance on how to navigate those major life changes and transitions while keeping your bipolar disorder in check.

First and foremost, it's important to recognize that life transitions can be particularly challenging for those of us with bipolar disorder. Our mood swings can be triggered by even the smallest of changes, so when faced with major life events, it's like throwing a stick of dynamite into an already volatile volcano. But fret not, my fellow bipolar warriors, for we have a secret weapon—preparation.

When it comes to managing bipolar disorder during life transitions, preparation is key. Think of it as packing your metaphorical suitcase with all the tools and strategies you'll need to weather the storm. So grab your mental passport and let's dive in!

One of the most important tools in your bipolar coping toolkit is self-care. It's like a magic potion that can help you navigate any storm that comes your way. So, during times of major life changes, make self-care your number one priority. Set aside time each day to do things that bring you joy and help you relax. Whether it's taking a bubble bath, going for a walk in nature, or indulging in a guilty pleasure (Netflix binge, anyone?), make sure you're taking care of yourself.

Another key strategy for managing bipolar disorder during life transitions is building a support system. Surround yourself with people who understand and support you. This could be friends, family, therapists, support groups — anyone who can offer a listening ear or a helping hand when you need it most. Remember, you don't have to face life's transitions alone. Reach out to your support system and let them be your rock.

Now, let's talk about the power of routine. Bipolar disorder loves routine like I love a good cup of coffee in the morning — it's essential. During times of major life changes, try to establish a routine that provides structure and stability. This can help stabilize your mood and make the transition smoother. So, set a schedule for yourself and stick to it as much as possible. And hey, if life throws you a curveball and disrupts your routine, just remember to be flexible and adapt. Life is full of surprises, after all.

Lastly, let's not forget about the importance of medication and therapy. During times of major life changes, it's crucial to stay on top of your treatment plan. Don't be afraid to reach out to your healthcare provider if you're experiencing any changes in symptoms or if you need additional support. Remember, they're there to help you navigate these transitions and find the right balance for your bipolar disorder.

So my friends, as we embark on this journey of coping with life transitions while managing bipolar disorder, remember that you are strong, resilient, and capable of weathering any storm that comes your way. With the right tools, strategies, and support, you can thrive in the ups and downs of life.

And hey, if all else fails, just remember to laugh. Because sometimes, a good dose of laughter is the best medicine for navigating life's transitions. So, my fellow bipolar warriors, let's face those twists and turns with a smile on our faces and a hearty laugh in our hearts. After all, we've got this — bipolar and all.

Chapter 6:
Thriving in Daily Life

Goal Setting and Time Management

In our fast-paced and ever-demanding world, it's easy to feel overwhelmed by the sheer number of tasks and responsibilities we have to juggle. From work deadlines to family obligations, it can often feel like there aren't enough hours in the day to get everything done. But fear not, my friends, for I am here to guide you on a journey towards setting realistic goals and managing your time effectively!

Now, let's start with goal setting. Setting goals is like embarking on a grand adventure. It gives us direction, purpose, and a sense of accomplishment when we finally reach our destination. But here's the thing, folks: goals need to be realistic. I know, I know, we all want to be superheroes and save the world within a single bound, but let's be honest: even Superman had his limits.

So, how do we set realistic goals? Well, it all starts with knowing ourselves. Take a good, hard look in the mirror and ask yourself, "What can I realistically achieve given my current circumstances?" You may be juggling a full-time job, a family, and a side hustle. Setting a goal to write the next great American novel in a month might not be the most realistic option. But hey, don't let that stop you from dreaming big! Just break it down into smaller, more manageable goals. You can commit to writing for an hour every day or completing a chapter every week. Remember, my friends, it's all about progress, not perfection.

Now, let's talk about time management. Ah, time, the great equalizer. We all have the same 24 hours in a day, but it's how we use those hours that truly matters. Time management is like a well-orchestrated symphony. It's all about finding the right balance, prioritizing tasks, and making the most of every precious moment.

One of my favorite time management techniques is the good ol' to-do list. It's like a roadmap for your day, guiding you from one task to the next. But here's a pro tip, folks: take your time with an endless list of tasks. Be selective, choose the most important ones, and tackle them with gusto. And hey, remember to reward yourself along the way. A little treat here and there never hurt anyone, right?

Another key aspect of time management is learning to say "no." I know it can be hard to turn down that extra project or social invitation, but sometimes, we have to prioritize our own well-being. Remember, my friends, you can't pour from an empty cup. So, don't be afraid to set boundaries and protect your time like a fierce mama bear protecting her cubs.

Now, all this talk about goal setting and time management can be overwhelming, but fear not! I've got a little joke to lighten the mood. Why did the scarecrow win an award? Because he was outstanding in his field! See, folks, even scarecrows, know the importance of setting goals and managing their time effectively.

In conclusion, my friends, goal setting and time management are the keys to unlocking a life of productivity and fulfillment. Remember to set realistic goals, break them down into manageable chunks, and make the most of your precious time. And hey, remember to laugh along the way. After all, humor goes a long way in making even the most daunting tasks more enjoyable. So go forth, my friends, and conquer the world one goal and minute at a time!

Building Resilience and Self-Compassion

Navigating the wild waves of bipolar disorder is no easy feat. It's like being caught in a storm at sea, with your emotions crashing against the rocks of your mind. But fear not, dear reader, for there is a lighthouse to guide you through these tumultuous waters - the beacon of resilience and self-compassion.

Resilience, my friends, is like a life raft in the storm. It is the ability to bounce back from adversity to withstand the waves of bipolar disorder without being swallowed whole. Think of it as your own personal superhero power, ready to swoop in and save the day when things get tough. And trust me, with bipolar disorder, things can get pretty darn tough.

How do we build this resilience? Well, it starts with a mindset shift. Instead of viewing bipolar disorder as a curse or a burden, we must see it as a challenge to overcome, an opportunity for growth. It's like that saying, "What doesn't kill you makes you stronger" - except in our case, it's more like, "What doesn't kill you makes you a freak in' superhero!"

But resilience alone is not enough. We must also cultivate self-compassion, the gentle hand that soothes our weary souls. Self-compassion is like a cozy blanket on a cold winter night, providing warmth and comfort when everything else feels cold and harsh. It is the act of treating ourselves with kindness, understanding, and forgiveness, even when our minds are racing, and our moods are swinging like a monkey on a trapeze.

Now, I know what you're thinking - "But how do I actually do all this?" Well, my friend, fear not, for I have some handy tips and tricks up my sleeve. First and foremost, we must practice self-care. This means taking the time to nurture ourselves physically, mentally, and emotionally. It could be as simple as taking a bubble bath, going for a walk-in nature, or indulging in our favorite hobbies. Whatever it is, make sure it brings you joy and replenishes your soul.

Secondly, we must surround ourselves with a support network of people who truly understand and accept us. These could be friends, family, or even support groups filled with fellow bipolar warriors. Having people who "get it" can make all the difference in the world, providing a safe space to share our struggles and triumphs without fear of judgment or stigma. Plus, they can also be a great source of laughter and comic relief - because, let's face it, sometimes we need a good ol' belly laugh to keep us sane.

And finally, we must learn to reframe our thoughts and beliefs about bipolar disorder. Instead of seeing it as a limitation, we can view it as a source of strength and resilience. After all, we have faced challenges that most people can only imagine, and we are still standing tall. We are the warriors, the fighters, the ones who refuse to let bipolar disorder define us. So, let's embrace our inner superhero and show the world just how resilient and compassionate we can be.

In conclusion, my fellow bipolar warriors, building resilience and self-compassion is the key to navigating the challenges of bipolar disorder. It is the life raft that keeps us afloat, the cozy blanket that wraps us in warmth. So, let us practice self-care, surround ourselves with a supportive network, and reframe our thoughts about bipolar disorder. And above all, let us embrace our inner superheroes and thrive in the ups and downs of life. After all, we are resilient, we are compassionate, and we are unstoppable. Now, go out there and conquer the world, my friends, one wave at a time!

Finding Meaning and Purpose

Exploring ways to find meaning and purpose in life despite the presence of bipolar disorder

Living with bipolar disorder can often feel like navigating a roller coaster ride. The ups and downs can be dizzying, leaving individuals feeling lost and unsure of their place in the world. However, it is important to remember that despite the challenges, it is possible to find meaning and purpose in life, even with bipolar disorder.

One of the first steps in finding meaning and purpose is to acknowledge and accept the presence of bipolar disorder. This may seem like an obvious point, but it is a crucial one. By accepting your condition, you are allowing yourself to move forward and take control of your life. It is important to remember that bipolar disorder does not define you as a person. You are so much more than your diagnosis.

Once you have accepted your condition, it is time to explore ways to find meaning and purpose in your life. One way to do this is by focusing on your strengths and passions. What are the things that bring you joy and make you feel alive? Is it painting, writing, or helping others? By identifying your strengths and passions, you can begin to build a life that aligns with your values and brings you fulfillment.

Another important aspect of finding meaning and purpose is setting goals. These goals can be big or small, but they should be meaningful to you. By setting goals, you are giving yourself something to work towards and a sense of direction. It is important to remember that these goals may change over time, and that's okay. Life is a journey, and it's okay to change course along the way.

Finding a support system is also crucial in the journey of finding meaning and purpose. Surrounding yourself with people who understand and support you can make all the difference. They can offer guidance, encouragement, and a listening ear when you need it most. Remember, you are not alone in this journey.

Humor can also be a powerful tool in finding meaning and purpose. While bipolar disorder is a serious condition, finding humor in certain situations can help lighten the load. Laughing at yourself and finding joy in the little things can bring a sense of perspective and resilience.

It is also important to remember that finding meaning and purpose is not a linear process. There will be ups and downs, setbacks and triumphs. But each step along the way is a part of your unique journey. Embrace the process, and trust that you are capable of finding meaning and purpose in your life.

Finding meaning and purpose in life despite the presence of bipolar disorder is possible. By accepting your condition, identifying your strengths and passions, setting goals, finding a support system, and embracing humor, you can create a life that is meaningful and fulfilling. Remember, you are more than your diagnosis. You are a resilient, capable individual who has the power to create a life filled with purpose and joy. So go out there and embrace the journey. And remember to laugh along the way. As they say, laughter is the best medicine - even for the ups and downs of bipolar disorder.

Creativity and Bipolar Disorder

Examining the Relationship and Harnessing Creative Outlets

When it comes to mental health, there are often unexpected connections that emerge. One such intriguing relationship is the link between bipolar disorder and creativity. As we dive into the depths of this fascinating connection, we will explore how bipolar disorder can both fuel and hinder creativity and, ultimately, how individuals can harness their creative outlets as a form of self-expression and healing.

The Dual Nature of Bipolar Disorder and Creativity:

Bipolar disorder, characterized by extreme mood swings, can be seen as a double-edged sword when it comes to creativity. On one hand, the manic episodes that often accompany bipolar disorder can be a breeding ground for wild ideas and unbridled imagination. The heightened energy and racing thoughts experienced during these episodes can lead to bursts of creativity that are both exhilarating and awe-inspiring.

On the other hand, the depressive episodes that follow can stifle creativity and drown the spark of inspiration. The weight of sadness and lack of motivation can make it challenging for individuals with bipolar disorder to tap into their creative wellsprings. It becomes a delicate dance between embracing the highs and managing the lows.

Navigating the Highs and Lows:

To truly harness the power of creativity in the face of bipolar disorder, it is crucial to understand and navigate the highs and lows that come with this condition. During manic episodes, it is essential to strike a balance between allowing creative ideas to flow freely and ensuring that they are grounded in reality. While grandiose visions may seem tempting, it is vital to evaluate the feasibility and practicality of these ideas.

Conversely, during depressive episodes, it is crucial to cultivate self-compassion and patience. Recognize that creativity may not flourish during these times, and that's okay. It is important to focus on self-care and finding solace in other forms of expression, such as journaling, painting, or simply taking long walks in nature. By nurturing oneself during these challenging moments, one can lay the groundwork for creativity to blossom once again.

The Healing Power of Creative Outlets:

Harnessing creative outlets can be a transformative tool in the journey of living with bipolar disorder. Engaging in creative activities not only provides an avenue for self-expression but also acts as a form of therapy. Through art, writing, music, or any other creative endeavor, individuals with bipolar disorder can channel their emotions, thoughts, and experiences into something tangible.

Creativity becomes a sanctuary, a safe space where the chaotic emotions of bipolar disorder can find solace and expression. It offers a means of communication that surpasses the limitations of words, allowing for a deeper connection with oneself and others. Whether it is a symphony composed during a manic episode or a painting that captures the essence of a depressive state, creative outlets become a testament to the strength and resilience of the human spirit.

Finding Balance:

While creativity can be a powerful tool in managing bipolar disorder, it is crucial to strike a balance between creativity and stability. It is essential to work alongside healthcare professionals to establish a treatment plan that addresses the unique needs of each individual. Medication, therapy, and lifestyle adjustments are all crucial components of maintaining stability and minimizing the disruptive effects of bipolar disorder.

However, it is equally important not to stifle creativity in the pursuit of stability. Encouraging open and honest communication with healthcare providers can help strike a delicate balance between managing bipolar disorder and embracing the creative spirit. With the right support system and a willingness to explore different avenues of expression, individuals with bipolar disorder can thrive creatively while maintaining their overall well-being.

Creativity and bipolar disorder have a complex and intertwined relationship. While bipolar disorder can both ignite and dampen creativity, individuals can harness their creative outlets as a form of self-expression and healing. By navigating the highs and lows, finding solace in creativity during difficult moments, and striking a balance between stability and artistic freedom, individuals with bipolar disorder can tap into the transformative power of creativity. Let us embrace the inherent beauty and complexity of this relationship and support those with bipolar disorder as they explore their creative journeys with humor, resilience, and a touch of whimsy. After all, life is a masterpiece in the making, and each stroke of creativity adds vibrancy to the canvas of existence.

Maintaining Stability and Preventing Relapse

Maintaining stability and preventing relapse are two critical aspects of managing bipolar disorder and living well with the condition. It's like walking a tightrope, constantly striving for balance while navigating the ups and downs. In this segment of the book, we will explore strategies for maintaining stability and preventing relapse through ongoing self-care and treatment adherence.

One of the fundamental pillars of stability is self-care. Taking care of yourself physically, emotionally, and mentally can help you stay grounded and resilient in the face of bipolar disorder's challenges. It's like putting on your oxygen mask before assisting others on a plane – you need to take care of yourself first.

So, what does self-care look like for someone with bipolar disorder? It can involve a variety of activities and practices that promote overall well-being. Regular exercise, for example, has been shown to have numerous benefits for mental health. Not only does it help regulate mood and reduce stress, but it also improves sleep and boosts self-esteem. Plus, who doesn't love the endorphin rush after a good workout? It's like a free ticket to the Happiness amusement park!

Another essential aspect of self-care is maintaining a healthy sleep routine. Bipolar disorder often disrupts sleep patterns, with episodes of mania or depression affecting both the quantity and quality of sleep. Establishing a consistent sleep schedule, practicing good sleep hygiene, and creating a relaxing bedtime routine can help regulate your sleep patterns and promote stability. Remember, sleep is not just for the weak; it's for the wise!

In addition to physical self-care, emotional and mental well-being are also vital for maintaining stability. This includes cultivating a strong support system – a team of people who understand and support you on your bipolar journey. Whether it's family, friends, therapists, or support groups, having a network of people who have your back can make a world of difference. They're like the Avengers of your mental health, ready to swoop in and save the day when you need them most.

Another crucial aspect of emotional and mental well-being is practicing stress management techniques. Bipolar disorder can be a rollercoaster ride of emotions, and stress can exacerbate symptoms and trigger episodes. Finding healthy coping mechanisms, such as deep breathing exercises, meditation, or engaging in hobbies that bring you joy and relaxation, can help reduce stress levels and promote stability. So, go ahead and indulge in that bubble bath or spend some quality time with your furry friend – they're excellent stress busters!

While self-care is a cornerstone of stability, it's equally important to adhere to your treatment plan. This means taking your medication as prescribed, attending therapy sessions, and actively participating in your mental health care. Treatment adherence is like sticking to a recipe – you need all the ingredients in the right proportions for the best results. So, don't skip those therapy sessions or play doctor by adjusting your medication without consulting your healthcare provider. They know what they're doing – after all, they went to medical school while you were busy binge-watching your favorite shows!

Moreover, it's essential to educate yourself about bipolar disorder and its management. Knowledge is power, and understanding your condition can empower you to take control of your mental health journey. Stay up to date with the latest research, read books (like this one!), and connect with reliable resources to expand your understanding. You're like a mental health detective, searching for clues and finding solutions to make your life better.

Remember, maintaining stability and preventing relapse is an ongoing process. It takes dedication, resilience, and a willingness to prioritize your well-being. But with self-care, treatment adherence, and a touch of humor along the way, you can thrive in the ups and downs of bipolar disorder. So, put on your cape, embrace your superpowers, and soar through life with stability and resilience. And don't forget to laugh – it's like medicine for the soul, and you're the funniest comedian in the bipolar universe!

Chapter 7:
Advocacy and Empowerment

-

Breaking the Stigma
We are encouraging individuals to share their stories and challenge the societal stigma surrounding bipolar disorder.
In a society that often shies away from discussions about mental health, breaking the stigma surrounding bipolar disorder can be an uphill battle. But it is a battle that we must fight for the sake of those who live with this condition and for the sake of a more compassionate and understanding society. In this segment of "Breaking the Stigma," we will explore the power of storytelling in challenging societal perceptions and encouraging individuals to share their experiences with bipolar disorder.
Storytelling has always been a powerful tool for human connection and understanding. When it comes to mental health, sharing personal stories can be a game-changer. By opening up about their struggles and triumphs, individuals with bipolar disorder can humanize their experiences and shed light on the often-misunderstood aspects of this condition.
One of the key reasons why storytelling is so effective in breaking the stigma surrounding bipolar disorder is its ability to challenge preconceived notions. When we hear someone's story, we see their humanity, their strength, and their resilience. We come to realize that bipolar disorder does not define a person, but rather, it is just one aspect of who they are. By sharing their stories, individuals with bipolar disorder can defy stereotypes and show the world that they are more than their diagnosis.
Another powerful aspect of storytelling is its ability to create empathy and understanding. When we hear someone's story, we are given a glimpse into their world. We can see the ups and downs, the struggles and the victories. Through storytelling, individuals with bipolar disorder can bridge the gap between themselves and those who may not understand their experiences. By sharing their stories, they invite others to walk in their shoes, if only for a moment, and develop a deeper sense of empathy and compassion.
However, breaking the stigma surrounding bipolar disorder requires more than just sharing personal stories. It also necessitates a societal shift in how we view and talk about mental health. We must create an environment where individuals feel safe and supported in sharing their experiences. This starts with education and awareness. By providing accurate information about bipolar disorder, we can dispel myths and misconceptions that contribute to the stigma.
Moreover, it is crucial to challenge the language we use when discussing mental health. Words like "crazy" or "insane" only perpetuate stereotypes and further isolate individuals with bipolar disorder. Instead, we must promote respectful and inclusive language that fosters understanding and support. Let's replace stigmatizing words with phrases like "living with bipolar disorder" or "managing bipolar disorder." Language has the power to shape perceptions, and by choosing our words carefully, we can contribute to a more accepting society.
Now, I don't know about you, but I've always found that a little humor goes a long way in breaking down barriers. So, here's a joke for you: Why did the bipolar bear go to therapy? Because he was tired of all the polarizing mood swings!
Jokes aside, the journey of breaking the stigma surrounding bipolar disorder is an ongoing one. It requires a collective effort from individuals, communities, and institutions. By encouraging individuals to share their stories, challenging societal perceptions, and promoting empathy and understanding, we can create a world where those with bipolar disorder are seen, heard, and supported.
In conclusion, storytelling is a powerful tool for breaking the stigma surrounding bipolar disorder. Through personal narratives, individuals can challenge preconceived notions, foster empathy, and

create a more compassionate society. By sharing their stories, they not only empower themselves but also pave the way for others to do the same. So, let's embrace the power of storytelling and work together to break the stigma surrounding bipolar disorder, one story at a time.

Advocating for Mental Health Rights

Empowering individuals to advocate for improved access to mental health resources and rights is a crucial step in creating a society that prioritizes the well-being of its citizens. It is a journey that requires dedication, perseverance, and a strong belief in the power of change. In this segment of the book, "Bipolar Women: Thriving in the Ups and Downs," we will delve into the importance of advocating for mental health rights and how individuals can take action to make a difference.

Advocating for mental health rights is not just about raising awareness; it is about actively working towards dismantling the barriers that prevent individuals from accessing the care and support they need. It is about fighting against the stigma surrounding mental health and demanding equal treatment and opportunities for everyone, regardless of their mental health condition. But where do we start?

The first step in advocating for improved access to mental health resources and rights is to educate ourselves. It is essential to understand the existing laws and policies that govern mental health care in our respective countries or regions. By familiarizing ourselves with the legal framework, we can identify the gaps and shortcomings that need to be addressed.

Once we have a solid understanding of the existing system, it's time to gather like-minded individuals who share our passion for mental health rights. Forming support groups or joining existing organizations can amplify our voices and increase our collective impact. Together, we can pool our resources, knowledge, and experiences to advocate for change on a larger scale.

Advocacy takes many forms, and each person has unique strengths and abilities to contribute. Some may choose to speak up at public forums, sharing personal stories and raising awareness about the challenges faced by individuals with mental health conditions. Others may prefer to engage with policymakers and government officials, lobbying for the implementation of comprehensive mental health policies. There are also opportunities to contribute through art, writing, or social media platforms, using creativity as a powerful tool for change.

Humor can also play a role in advocacy, helping to break down barriers and engage a wider audience. Mental health is often seen as a taboo topic, but by injecting humor into our conversations, we can create a more open and accepting environment. For example, we can use jokes to highlight the absurdity of stigma or to challenge misconceptions about mental health. Humor allows us to approach difficult subjects with a lighter touch while still conveying a powerful message.

One of the most effective ways to advocate for mental health rights is by sharing our stories. Personal narratives have a unique ability to humanize the issue, making it relatable and compelling. By sharing our experiences, we can challenge stereotypes and misconceptions, fostering empathy and understanding among the general public. Our stories can inspire others to speak up, seek help, and become advocates themselves.

In the fight for improved access to mental health resources and rights, it is crucial to remember that change does not happen overnight. It requires persistence, resilience, and a commitment to the cause. Advocacy is not always easy, but the rewards are immeasurable. By empowering individuals to advocate for mental health rights, we can create a society that values and supports the well-being of all its members.

So, let's join forces armed with knowledge, humor, and a passion for change. Let's raise our voices and advocate for improved access to mental health resources and rights. Together, we can make a difference and create a world where mental health is not just a priority but a fundamental right. As the saying goes, "If you want to go fast, go alone. If you want to go far, go together." Let's go far together

Supporting Others with bipolar disorder

Offering Guidance and Resources for a Fulfilling Life

Living with bipolar disorder can be challenging, but with the right support and resources, individuals can thrive and lead fulfilling lives. In this segment of the book, we will explore how to provide guidance and resources to others living with bipolar disorder. Whether you are a friend, family member, or healthcare professional, your role in supporting someone with bipolar disorder is crucial. So, let's dive in and learn how to make a positive impact!

Understanding Bipolar Disorder:

Before offering support, it's important to have a solid understanding of bipolar disorder. Bipolar disorder is a mental health condition characterized by extreme mood swings, ranging from manic highs to depressive lows. These mood swings can disrupt daily life and relationships, making it essential to provide the right support.

1. Be an Active Listener:

One of the most powerful ways to support someone with bipolar disorder is by being an active listener. Allow them to express their thoughts, emotions, and concerns without judgment. Please give them your undivided attention and validate their experiences. Remember, it's not about offering solutions but providing a safe space for them to be heard.

2. Educate Yourself:

To offer the best support, educate yourself about bipolar disorder. Read books, attend support groups, and seek information from reputable sources. By understanding the symptoms, treatment options, and challenges associated with bipolar disorder, you can provide informed guidance and resources.

3. Encourage Professional Help:

While your support is invaluable, it's crucial to encourage the individual to seek professional help. Bipolar disorder often requires a comprehensive treatment plan involving therapy, medication, and lifestyle adjustments. Be a source of encouragement and offer assistance in finding qualified healthcare professionals.

4. Foster a Supportive Network:

Supporting someone with bipolar disorder is not a one-person job. Encourage the individual to build a support network that includes family, friends, and support groups. Connecting with others who have similar experiences can provide a sense of community, understanding, and shared resources.

5. Promote Healthy Lifestyle Choices:

A healthy lifestyle plays a significant role in managing bipolar disorder. Encourage the individual to prioritize regular exercise, balanced nutrition, and sufficient sleep. Help them establish healthy routines and assist in finding activities they enjoy, such as yoga, hiking, or painting, as these can serve as therapeutic outlets.

6. Monitor Medication Compliance:

If the individual is taking medication to manage their bipolar disorder, it's important to support them in maintaining compliance. Offer reminders, assist with medication management tools, and be a sounding board for any concerns or side effects they may experience.

7. Help Identify Triggers and Warning Signs:

Bipolar disorder often has triggers and warning signs that can precede mood swings. Support the individual in identifying these triggers and warning signs, as early intervention can prevent or lessen the severity of episodes. Please encourage them to keep a mood journal and establish coping strategies to manage these situations.

8. Celebrate Accomplishments:

Living with bipolar disorder is not easy, so it's important to celebrate every accomplishment, big or small. Acknowledge their efforts, resilience, and progress. Be their cheerleader, reminding them of how far they've come and inspiring them to keep moving forward.

Supporting others with bipolar disorder requires empathy, understanding, and a commitment to their well-being. By being an active listener, educating yourself, encouraging professional help, fostering a supportive network, promoting healthy lifestyle choices, monitoring medication compliance, helping identify triggers and warning signs, and celebrating accomplishments, you can make a significant positive impact on their journey towards a fulfilling life.

Remember, supporting someone with bipolar disorder is not about "fixing" them; it's about offering guidance, resources, and love. So, let's be there for them, cheer them on, and help them navigate the ups and downs of bipolar disorder with strength and resilience. Together, we can make a difference! And hey, remember to laugh along the way because humor is the best medicine, even when dealing with serious topics like bipolar disorder.

Creating a Supportive Community

When it comes to living with bipolar disorder, one of the most crucial elements of managing and thriving is having a strong support system. Building a supportive community of individuals who understand what it's like to navigate the ups and downs of bipolar disorder can make all the difference in the world. It's like having a squad of superheroes by your side, ready to leap into action when you need them the most. So, let's dive into the importance of creating a supportive community and how to go about it.

First things first, let's address the elephant in the room - bipolar disorder can be tough. We all know it. But hey, life is all about finding the silver linings, right? And one of those silver linings is the opportunity to connect with others who are going through similar experiences. Trust me, there's nothing quite like bonding over mood swings and medication side effects to bring people together. It's like a secret club, except the membership fee is a little higher than your average book club.

Now, how exactly does a supportive community help? Well, picture this: you're having a particularly rough day, feeling like you're riding an emotional rollercoaster with no brakes. Who do you turn to for support? Your mom? Your best friend? Well, those are great options, but having a community of individuals who truly understand what you're going through adds a whole new level of comfort and understanding.

In a supportive community, you can share your experiences, fears, and victories without fear of judgment. These are the people who get it, who understand the intricacies of bipolar disorder, and who can offer invaluable advice and empathy. They've been there, done that, and have the mood chart to prove it. Plus, let's be honest, who better to ask for tips on finding the perfect therapist or navigating the medication maze than someone who has been through it themselves?

Now, building a supportive community takes time to happen. It takes time, effort, and a sprinkle of social skills. So, let's break it down into a few simple steps to get you started:

Step 1: Seek out support groups. These can be in-person or online, depending on your comfort level and location. Trust me, there's a group for everything these days - from early birds who want to conquer the world at 4 am to night owls who can't fall asleep until 4 am.

Step 2: Engage in conversations. Feel free to share your story and ask questions. Remember, vulnerability is not a weakness; it's a superpower. Plus, you never know; you might meet your bipolar BFF, who shares your love for puns and penguins.

Step 3: Be an active participant. Don't just lurk in the shadows like a ninja with a smartphone. Engage, offer support, and be the superhero you've always wanted to be. Remember, kindness and compassion are contagious.

Step 4: Take it offline. Once you've established connections online, why not take the leap and meet up in person? Grab a cup of coffee, go for a walk, or organize a pizza party. The possibilities are endless, just like your potential for building meaningful friendships.

And remember, in this supportive community, laughter is the best medicine. So, let's lighten the mood with a joke, shall we?

Creating a supportive community of individuals with bipolar disorder is not just about finding people who understand your struggles but also about building a network of love, laughter, and shared experiences. So, go out there, find your tribe, and together, let's thrive in the ups and downs of bipolar disorder!

Chapter 8:
Reflecting on the Journey

As you turn the pages of this book, taking in the wealth of knowledge and experiences shared, it's important to take a moment to reflect on your own personal journey with bipolar disorder. This journey has been a rollercoaster ride, with its ups and downs, twists and turns. But through it all, you have grown and evolved into the resilient person you are today.

Reflecting on your journey allows you to acknowledge the progress you've made, the challenges you've overcome, and the strength you've discovered within yourself. It's a chance to celebrate your victories, no matter how small they may seem, and to give yourself credit for the hard work and determination it took to get where you are today.

Take a moment to close your eyes and think back to the beginning of your journey. Remember the confusion and fear you felt when you were first diagnosed—the uncertainty of what the future holds and the doubts that creep into your mind. But also remember the glimmers of hope that shone through, the support of loved ones, and the knowledge that you were not alone.

Now, fast forward to the present moment. Think about the progress you've made in managing your bipolar disorder. Perhaps you've found the right combination of medications that help stabilize your moods. Maybe you've developed coping mechanisms and strategies that allow you to navigate the ups and downs with more grace and ease. Or it could be that you've sought therapy and counseling and have gained valuable insights and tools to manage your mental health.

No matter where you are in your journey, it's important to acknowledge and celebrate your growth. Bipolar disorder is not an easy road to travel, but you have shown incredible resilience and strength in facing the challenges that come with it. You are a warrior, and your journey is a testament to your courage and determination.

So, as you read through the pages of this book, take the time to reflect on your own personal journey. Pause after each chapter and ask yourself how the information and insights shared resonate with your own experiences. Take note of the progress you've made, the lessons you've learned, and the ways in which you have grown.

And remember, you are not alone on this journey. There are countless others who have walked, and continue to walk, the same path as you. Reach out for support when you need it, and offer support to others when you can. Together, we can thrive in the ups and downs of bipolar disorder and live well despite the challenges we face.

Now, let's dive into the pages of this book and continue our journey of understanding, managing, and living well with bipolar disorder. But remember to pause every now and then, reflect on your own personal growth, and give yourself a pat on the back for how far you've come. And hey, remember, laughter is the best medicine, so remember to sprinkle in a few jokes along the way. After all, a little humor can go a long way in brightening even the darkest of days.

Moving Forward with Resilience
Final Thoughts on Leading a Fulfilling Life Despite the Challenges of Bipolar Disorder

Life is unpredictable, filled with highs and lows that can make it feel like a rollercoaster ride. But for those of us living with bipolar disorder, this ride can be even more intense, with twists and turns that can leave us feeling disoriented and overwhelmed. Yet, amidst the chaos, there is hope. In the face of bipolar disorder, resilience becomes our secret weapon, empowering us to move forward and lead fulfilling lives.

Resilience is not a magical quality that only a select few possess. It is a skill that can be cultivated and honed over time. Just like a muscle, the more we exercise resilience, the stronger it becomes. It is through resilience that we find the strength to persevere, to weather the storms that bipolar disorder may throw our way.

So, how do we cultivate resilience? It starts with self-awareness. Understanding our triggers, our patterns, and our limits allows us to navigate the ups and downs with greater ease. It's like having a compass that guides us through the darkest of times, reminding us of our inner strength and ability to overcome.

But resilience is not just about weathering the storm; it's also about embracing the sunshine. It's about finding joy and fulfillment in the little moments, even amidst the challenges of bipolar disorder. It's about celebrating our victories, no matter how small they may seem. Whether it's getting out of bed on a difficult day or accomplishing a long-term goal, each step forward is a testament to our resilience.

One key aspect of leading a fulfilling life with bipolar disorder is the importance of support. We are not alone in this journey, and reaching out to others who understand can make a world of difference. Whether it's through therapy, support groups, or simply having a trusted friend or family member to lean on, having a strong support system can provide the foundation we need to move forward with resilience.

But resilience is not just about bouncing back; it's about bouncing forward. It's about embracing the challenges as opportunities for growth and transformation. It's about learning from our experiences and using them to become stronger, wiser, and more compassionate individuals.

Now, I know that living with bipolar disorder is no laughing matter, but sometimes, a little humor can go a long way in lightening the load. Laughter is a form of resilience in itself, a reminder that even in the darkest of times, there is still lightness and joy to be found.

So, my friends, as we come to the end of this journey together, let us remember that resilience is not just about surviving; it's about thriving. It's about embracing the challenges, finding support, and never giving up. It's about living a life that is not defined by bipolar disorder but by our strength, resilience, and ability to find joy amidst the ups and downs.

As we move forward with resilience, let us hold our heads high, knowing that we are capable of leading fulfilling lives despite the challenges we face. Let us embrace the journey, with all its twists and turns, and find solace in the fact that we are not alone. Together, we can move mountains and defy the odds.

So, my dear readers, go forth with resilience in your hearts and a smile on your face. The world is waiting for you to shine.

Continuing the Journey

After journeying through the ups and downs of bipolar disorder with me, you might be wondering, "Where do I go from here?" Well, fear not, my fellow bipolar women! While this book has provided you with a comprehensive guide to understanding, managing, and living well with bipolar disorder, there is still so much more to explore and learn on this ongoing journey.

First and foremost, it's crucial to recognize that this book is just the beginning. It's like the appetizer to a delicious feast of knowledge and support that awaits you. There are countless resources available to help you further navigate the complexities of bipolar disorder and continue your growth toward thriving in every aspect of your life.

One valuable resource that I highly recommend is support groups. These communities of individuals who understand firsthand the challenges of bipolar disorder can provide a safe space for you to share your experiences, seek advice, and find solace in the company of others who truly get it. Plus, you might even make some new friends along the way! Just be prepared for the occasional questionable potluck dish – we all have our culinary quirks.

Additionally, therapy is an essential tool for ongoing support and growth. A skilled therapist can help you navigate the emotional and psychological aspects of bipolar disorder, providing guidance and

coping strategies tailored specifically to your unique needs. Think of them as your personal cheerleader, ready to help you tackle any hurdles that may come your way. And remember, therapy doesn't have to be all serious and somber – a good therapist knows how to sprinkle a little humor into the mix to lighten the mood.
In the realm of self-help literature, there is a plethora of books out there that can provide further insights and practical strategies for managing bipolar disorder. From memoirs by individuals who have triumphed over their own struggles to workbooks that offer exercises and tools for self-reflection, there is something for everyone. Just be warned, some of these books may be as thick as a phone book – but don't worry, they're much more interesting!

For those who prefer a more modern approach, technology has opened up a world of possibilities. There are numerous apps available that can help you track your moods, manage medication schedules, and even provide guided meditations and relaxation exercises. It's like having a pocket-sized therapist right at your fingertips – although I must admit, they're not great at giving high fives.
And finally, always appreciate the power of a strong support system. Surround yourself with friends and family who understand and accept you, quirks and all. These are the people who will be there for you through the highs and lows, providing a shoulder to lean on and a listening ear. And hey, they might even bring you a latte when you're feeling particularly down – now that's true friendship.
So, my dear bipolar women, as you continue your journey beyond the pages of this book, remember that there is a world of resources and support waiting for you. Embrace the opportunities to learn, grow, and connect with others who share your experiences. And most importantly, never forget to laugh along the way – after all, humor is the best medicine, right? Now go forth, my fellow thrivers, and conquer the world with your resilient spirit and infectious laughter!

Chapter   6:
Thriving in Daily Life

Goal Setting and Time Management

In our fast-paced and ever-demanding world, it's easy to feel overwhelmed by the sheer number of tasks and responsibilities we have to juggle. From work deadlines to family obligations, it can often feel like there simply aren't enough hours in the day to get everything done. But fear not, my friends, for I am here to guide you on a journey towards setting realistic goals and managing your time effectively!

Now, let's start with goal setting. Setting goals is like embarking on a grand adventure. It gives us direction, purpose, and a sense of accomplishment when we finally reach our destination. But here's the thing, folks: goals need to be realistic. I know, I know, we all want to be superheroes and save the world in a single bound, but let's be honest, even Superman had his limits.

So, how do we set realistic goals? Well, it all starts with knowing ourselves. Take a good, hard look in the mirror and ask yourself, "What can I realistically achieve given my current circumstances?" Maybe you're juggling a full-time job, a family, and a side hustle. In that case, setting a goal to write the next great American novel in a month might not be the most realistic option. But hey, don't let that stop you from dreaming big! Just break it down into smaller, more manageable goals. Maybe you can commit to writing for an hour every day or completing a chapter every week. Remember, my friends, it's all about progress, not perfection.

Now, let's talk about time management. Ah, time, the great equalizer. We all have the same 24 hours in a day, but it's how we use those hours that truly matters. Time management is like a well-orchestrated symphony. It's all about finding the right balance, prioritizing tasks, and making the most of every precious moment.

One of my favorite time management techniques is the good ol' to-do list. It's like a roadmap for your day, guiding you from one task to the next. But here's a pro tip, folks: don't overwhelm yourself with an endless list of tasks. Be selective, choose the most important ones, and tackle them with gusto. And hey, don't forget to reward yourself along the way. A little treat here and there never hurt anyone, right?

Another key aspect of time management is learning to say "no." I know, it can be hard to turn down that extra project or social invitation, but sometimes we have to prioritize our own well-being. Remember, my friends, you can't pour from an empty cup. So, don't be afraid to set boundaries and protect your time like a fierce mama bear protecting her cubs.

Now, I know all this talk about goal setting and time management can be a bit overwhelming, but fear not! I've got a little joke to lighten the mood. Why did the scarecrow win an award? Because he was outstanding in his field! See, folks, even scarecrows know the importance of setting goals and managing their time effectively.

In conclusion, my friends, goal setting and time management are the keys to unlocking a life of productivity and fulfillment. Remember to set realistic goals, break them down into manageable chunks, and make the most of your precious time. And hey, don't forget to laugh along the way. After all, a little humor goes a long way in making even the most daunting tasks a little more enjoyable. So go forth, my friends, and conquer the world one goal and minute at a time!

Building Resilience and Self-Compassion

Navigating the wild waves of bipolar disorder is no easy feat. It's like being caught in a storm at sea, with your emotions crashing against the rocks of your mind. But fear not, dear reader, for there is a lighthouse to guide you through these tumultuous waters – the beacon of resilience and self-compassion.

Resilience, my friends, is like a life raft in the storm. It is the ability to bounce back from adversity, to withstand the waves of bipolar disorder without being swallowed whole. Think of it as your own personal superhero power, ready to swoop in and save the day when things get tough. And trust me, with bipolar disorder, things can get pretty darn tough.

So how do we build this resilience, you may ask? Well, it starts with a mindset shift. Instead of viewing bipolar disorder as a curse or a burden, we must see it as a challenge to overcome, an opportunity for growth. It's like that saying, "What doesn't kill you makes you stronger" - except in our case, it's more like, "What doesn't kill you makes you a freakin' superhero!"

But resilience alone is not enough. We must also cultivate self-compassion, the gentle hand that soothes our weary souls. Self-compassion is like a cozy blanket on a cold winter's night, providing warmth and comfort when everything else feels cold and harsh. It is the act of treating ourselves with kindness, understanding, and forgiveness, even when our minds are racing and our moods are swinging like a monkey on a trapeze.

Now, I know what you're thinking - "But how do I actually do all this?" Well, my friend, fear not, for I have some handy tips and tricks up my sleeve. First and foremost, we must practice self-care. This means taking the time to nurture ourselves, physically, mentally, and emotionally. It could be as simple as taking a bubble bath, going for a walk in nature, or indulging in our favorite hobbies. Whatever it is, make sure it brings you joy and replenishes your soul.

Secondly, we must surround ourselves with a support network of people who truly understand and accept us. These could be friends, family, or even support groups filled with fellow bipolar warriors. Having people who "get it" can make all the difference in the world, providing a safe space to share our struggles and triumphs without fear of judgment or stigma. Plus, they can also be a great source of laughter and comic relief - because let's face it, sometimes we just need a good ol' belly laugh to keep us sane.

And finally, we must learn to reframe our thoughts and beliefs about bipolar disorder. Instead of seeing it as a limitation, we can view it as a source of strength and resilience. After all, we have faced challenges that most people can only imagine, and we are still standing tall. We are the warriors, the fighters, the ones who refuse to let bipolar disorder define us. So let's embrace our inner superhero and show the world just how resilient and compassionate we can be.

In conclusion, my fellow bipolar warriors, building resilience and self-compassion is the key to navigating the challenges of bipolar disorder. It is the life raft that keeps us afloat, the cozy blanket that wraps us in warmth. So let us practice self-care, surround ourselves with a supportive network, and reframe our thoughts about bipolar disorder. And above all, let us embrace our inner superhero and thrive in the ups and downs of life. After all, we are resilient, we are compassionate, and we are unstoppable. Now go out there and conquer the world, my friends, one wave at a time!

Finding Meaning and Purpose

Exploring ways to find meaning and purpose in life despite the presence of bipolar disorder

Living with bipolar disorder can often feel like navigating a roller coaster ride. The ups and downs can be dizzying, leaving individuals feeling lost and unsure of their place in the world. However, it is important to remember that despite the challenges, it is possible to find meaning and purpose in life even with bipolar disorder.

One of the first steps in finding meaning and purpose is to acknowledge and accept the presence of bipolar disorder. This may seem like an obvious point, but it is a crucial one. By accepting your condition, you are allowing yourself to move forward and take control of your life. It is important to remember that bipolar disorder does not define you as a person. You are so much more than your diagnosis.

Once you have accepted your condition, it is time to explore ways to find meaning and purpose in your life. One way to do this is by focusing on your strengths and passions. What are the things that bring you joy and make you feel alive? Is it painting, writing, or perhaps helping others? By identifying your strengths and passions, you can begin to build a life that aligns with your values and brings you fulfillment.

Another important aspect of finding meaning and purpose is setting goals. These goals can be big or small, but they should be meaningful to you. By setting goals, you are giving yourself something to work towards and a sense of direction. It is important to remember that these goals may change over time, and that's okay. Life is a journey, and it's okay to change course along the way.

Finding a support system is also crucial in the journey of finding meaning and purpose. Surrounding yourself with people who understand and support you can make all the difference. They can offer guidance, encouragement, and a listening ear when you need it most. Remember, you are not alone in this journey.

Humor can also be a powerful tool in finding meaning and purpose. While bipolar disorder is a serious condition, finding the humor in certain situations can help lighten the load. Laughing at yourself and finding joy in the little things can bring a sense of perspective and resilience.

It is also important to remember that finding meaning and purpose is not a linear process. There will be ups and downs, setbacks and triumphs. But each step along the way is a part of your unique journey. Embrace the process, and trust that you are capable of finding meaning and purpose in your life.

Finding meaning and purpose in life despite the presence of bipolar disorder is possible. By accepting your condition, identifying your strengths and passions, setting goals, finding a support system, and embracing humor, you can create a life that is meaningful and fulfilling. Remember, you are more than your diagnosis. You are a resilient, capable individual who has the power to create a life filled with purpose and joy. So go out there and embrace the journey. And don't forget to laugh along the way. As they say, laughter is the best medicine – even for the ups and downs of bipolar disorder.

Creativity and Bipolar Disorder

Examining the Relationship and Harnessing Creative Outlets

When it comes to mental health, there are often unexpected connections that emerge. One such intriguing relationship is the link between bipolar disorder and creativity. As we dive into the depths of this fascinating connection, we will explore how bipolar disorder can both fuel and hinder creativity, and ultimately, how individuals can harness their creative outlets as a form of self-expression and healing.

The Dual Nature of Bipolar Disorder and Creativity:

Bipolar disorder, characterized by extreme mood swings, can be seen as a double-edged sword when it comes to creativity. On one hand, the manic episodes that often accompany bipolar disorder can be a breeding ground for wild ideas and unbridled imagination. The heightened energy and racing thoughts experienced during these episodes can lead to bursts of creativity that are both exhilarating and awe-inspiring.

On the other hand, the depressive episodes that follow can stifle creativity and drown the spark of inspiration. The weight of sadness and lack of motivation can make it challenging for individuals with bipolar disorder to tap into their creative wellspring. It becomes a delicate dance between embracing the highs and managing the lows.

Navigating the Highs and Lows:

To truly harness the power of creativity in the face of bipolar disorder, it is crucial to understand and navigate the highs and lows that come with this condition. During manic episodes, it is essential to strike a balance between allowing the creative ideas to flow freely and ensuring that they are grounded in reality. While grandiose visions may seem tempting, it is vital to evaluate the feasibility and practicality of these ideas.

Conversely, during depressive episodes, it is crucial to cultivate self-compassion and patience. Recognize that creativity may not flourish during these times, and that's okay. It is important to focus on self-care and finding solace in other forms of expression, such as journaling, painting, or simply taking long walks in nature. By nurturing oneself during these challenging moments, one can lay the groundwork for creativity to blossom once again.

The Healing Power of Creative Outlets:

Harnessing creative outlets can be a transformative tool in the journey of living with bipolar disorder. Engaging in creative activities not only provides an avenue for self-expression but also acts as a form of therapy. Through art, writing, music, or any other creative endeavor, individuals with bipolar disorder can channel their emotions, thoughts, and experiences into something tangible.

Creativity becomes a sanctuary, a safe space where the chaotic emotions of bipolar disorder can find solace and expression. It offers a means of communication that surpasses the limitations of words, allowing for a deeper connection with oneself and others. Whether it is a symphony composed during a manic episode or a painting that captures the essence of a depressive state, creative outlets become a testament to the strength and resilience of the human spirit.

Finding Balance:

While creativity can be a powerful tool in managing bipolar disorder, it is crucial to strike a balance between creativity and stability. It is essential to work alongside healthcare professionals to establish a treatment plan that addresses the unique needs of each individual. Medication, therapy, and lifestyle adjustments are all crucial components of maintaining stability and minimizing the disruptive effects of bipolar disorder.

However, it is equally important not to stifle creativity in the pursuit of stability. Encouraging open and honest communication with healthcare providers can help strike a delicate balance between managing bipolar disorder and embracing the creative spirit. With the right support system and a willingness to explore different avenues of expression, individuals with bipolar disorder can thrive creatively while maintaining their overall well-being.

Creativity and bipolar disorder have a complex and intertwined relationship. While bipolar disorder can both ignite and dampen creativity, individuals can harness their creative outlets as a form of self-expression and healing. By navigating the highs and lows, finding solace in creativity during difficult moments, and striking a balance between stability and artistic freedom, individuals with bipolar disorder can tap into the transformative power of creativity. Let us embrace the inherent beauty and complexity of this relationship, and support those with bipolar disorder as they explore their creative journeys with humor, resilience, and a touch of whimsy. After all, life is a masterpiece in the making, and each stroke of creativity adds vibrancy to the canvas of existence.

Maintaining Stability and Preventing Relapse

Maintaining stability and preventing relapse are two critical aspects of managing bipolar disorder and living well with the condition. It's like walking a tightrope, constantly striving for balance while navigating the ups and downs. In this segment of the book, we will explore strategies for maintaining stability and preventing relapse through ongoing self-care and treatment adherence.

One of the fundamental pillars of stability is self-care. Taking care of yourself physically, emotionally, and mentally can help you stay grounded and resilient in the face of bipolar disorder's challenges. It's like putting on your oxygen mask before assisting others on a plane — you need to take care of yourself first.

So, what does self-care look like for someone with bipolar disorder? It can involve a variety of activities and practices that promote overall well-being. Regular exercise, for example, has been shown to have numerous benefits for mental health. Not only does it help regulate mood and reduce stress, but it also improves sleep and boosts self-esteem. Plus, who doesn't love the endorphin rush after a good workout? It's like a free ticket to the happiness amusement park!

Another essential aspect of self-care is maintaining a healthy sleep routine. Bipolar disorder often disrupts sleep patterns, with episodes of mania or depression affecting both the quantity and quality of sleep. Establishing a consistent sleep schedule, practicing good sleep hygiene, and creating a relaxing bedtime routine can help regulate your sleep patterns and promote stability. Remember, sleep is not just for the weak; it's for the wise!

In addition to physical self-care, emotional and mental well-being are also vital for maintaining stability. This includes cultivating a strong support system — a team of people who understand and support you on your bipolar journey. Whether it's family, friends, therapists, or support groups, having a network of people who have your back can make a world of difference. They're like the Avengers of your mental health, ready to swoop in and save the day when you need them most.

Another crucial aspect of emotional and mental well-being is practicing stress management techniques. Bipolar disorder can be a rollercoaster ride of emotions, and stress can exacerbate symptoms and trigger episodes. Finding healthy coping mechanisms, such as deep breathing exercises, meditation, or engaging in hobbies that bring you joy and relaxation, can help reduce stress levels and promote stability. So, go ahead and indulge in that bubble bath or spend some quality time with your furry friend — they're excellent stress busters!

While self-care is a cornerstone of stability, it's equally important to adhere to your treatment plan. This means taking your medication as prescribed, attending therapy sessions, and actively participating in your mental health care. Treatment adherence is like sticking to a recipe — you need all the ingredients in the right proportions for the best results. So, don't skip those therapy sessions or play doctor by adjusting your medication without consulting your healthcare provider. They know what they're doing — after all, they went to medical school while you were busy binge-watching your favorite shows!

Moreover, it's essential to educate yourself about bipolar disorder and its management. Knowledge is power, and understanding your condition can empower you to take control of your mental health journey. Stay up to date with the latest research, read books (like this one!), and connect with reliable resources to expand your understanding. You're like a mental health detective, searching for clues and finding solutions to make your life better.

Remember, maintaining stability and preventing relapse is an ongoing process. It takes dedication, resilience, and a willingness to prioritize your well-being. But with self-care, treatment adherence, and a touch of humor along the way, you can thrive in the ups and downs of bipolar disorder. So, put on your cape, embrace your superpowers, and soar through life with stability and resilience. And don't forget to laugh — it's like medicine for the soul, and you're the funniest comedian in the bipolar universe!

Chapter 7:
Advocacy and Empowerment

Breaking the Stigma

Encouraging individuals to share their stories and challenge societal stigma surrounding bipolar disorder.

In a society that often shies away from discussions about mental health, breaking the stigma surrounding bipolar disorder can be an uphill battle. But it is a battle that we must fight, for the sake of those who live with this condition and for the sake of a more compassionate and understanding society. In this segment of "Breaking the Stigma," we will explore the power of storytelling in challenging societal perceptions and encouraging individuals to share their experiences with bipolar disorder.

Storytelling has always been a powerful tool for human connection and understanding. When it comes to mental health, sharing personal stories can be a game-changer. By opening up about their struggles and triumphs, individuals with bipolar disorder can humanize their experiences and shed light on the often-misunderstood aspects of this condition.

One of the key reasons why storytelling is so effective in breaking the stigma surrounding bipolar disorder is its ability to challenge preconceived notions. When we hear someone's story, we see their humanity, their strength, and their resilience. We come to realize that bipolar disorder does not define a person, but rather, it is just one aspect of who they are. By sharing their stories, individuals with bipolar disorder can defy stereotypes and show the world that they are more than their diagnosis.

Another powerful aspect of storytelling is its ability to create empathy and understanding. When we hear someone's story, we are given a glimpse into their world. We can see the ups and downs, the struggles and the victories. Through storytelling, individuals with bipolar disorder can bridge the gap between themselves and those who may not understand their experiences. By sharing their stories, they invite others to walk in their shoes, if only for a moment, and develop a deeper sense of empathy and compassion.

However, breaking the stigma surrounding bipolar disorder requires more than just sharing personal stories. It also necessitates a societal shift in how we view and talk about mental health. We must create an environment where individuals feel safe and supported in sharing their experiences. This starts with education and awareness. By providing accurate information about bipolar disorder, we can dispel myths and misconceptions that contribute to the stigma.

Moreover, it is crucial to challenge the language we use when discussing mental health. Words like "crazy" or "insane" only perpetuate stereotypes and further isolate individuals with bipolar disorder. Instead, we must promote respectful and inclusive language that fosters understanding and support.

Let's replace stigmatizing words with phrases like "living with bipolar disorder" or "managing bipolar disorder." Language has the power to shape perceptions, and by choosing our words carefully, we can contribute to a more accepting society.

Now, I don't know about you, but I've always found that a little humor goes a long way in breaking down barriers. So, here's a joke for you: Why did the bipolar bear go to therapy? Because he was tired of all the polar-izing mood swings!

Jokes aside, the journey of breaking the stigma surrounding bipolar disorder is an ongoing one. It requires a collective effort from individuals, communities, and institutions. By encouraging individuals to share their stories, challenging societal perceptions, and promoting empathy and understanding, we can create a world where those with bipolar disorder are seen, heard, and supported.

In conclusion, storytelling is a powerful tool in breaking the stigma surrounding bipolar disorder. Through personal narratives, individuals can challenge preconceived notions, foster empathy, and create a more compassionate society. By sharing their stories, they not only empower themselves but also pave the way for others to do the same. So, let's embrace the power of storytelling and work together to break the stigma surrounding bipolar disorder, one story at a time.

Advocating for Mental Health Rights

Empowering individuals to advocate for improved access to mental health resources and rights is a crucial step in creating a society that prioritizes the well-being of its citizens. It is a journey that requires dedication, perseverance, and a strong belief in the power of change. In this segment of the book, "Bipolar Women: Thriving in the Ups and Downs," we will delve into the importance of advocating for mental health rights and how individuals can take action to make a difference.

Advocating for mental health rights is not just about raising awareness; it is about actively working towards dismantling the barriers that prevent individuals from accessing the care and support they need. It is about fighting against the stigma surrounding mental health and demanding equal treatment and opportunities for everyone, regardless of their mental health condition. But where do we start?

The first step in advocating for improved access to mental health resources and rights is to educate ourselves. It is essential to understand the existing laws and policies that govern mental health care in our respective countries or regions. By familiarizing ourselves with the legal framework, we can identify the gaps and shortcomings that need to be addressed.

Once we have a solid understanding of the existing system, it's time to gather like-minded individuals who share our passion for mental health rights. Forming support groups or joining existing organizations can amplify our voices and increase our collective impact. Together, we can pool our resources, knowledge, and experiences to advocate for change on a larger scale.

Advocacy takes many forms, and each person has unique strengths and abilities to contribute. Some may choose to speak up at public forums, sharing personal stories and raising awareness about the challenges faced by individuals with mental health conditions. Others may prefer to engage with policymakers and government officials, lobbying for the implementation of comprehensive mental health policies. There are also opportunities to contribute through art, writing, or social media platforms, using creativity as a powerful tool for change.

Humor can also play a role in advocacy, helping to break down barriers and engage a wider audience. Mental health is often seen as a taboo topic, but by injecting humor into our conversations, we can create a more open and accepting environment. For example, we can use jokes to highlight the absurdity of stigma or to challenge misconceptions about mental health. Humor allows us to approach difficult subjects with a lighter touch while still conveying a powerful message.

One of the most effective ways to advocate for mental health rights is by sharing our stories. Personal narratives have a unique ability to humanize the issue, making it relatable and compelling. By sharing our experiences, we can challenge stereotypes and misconceptions, fostering empathy and understanding among the general public. Our stories can inspire others to speak up, seek help, and become advocates themselves.

In the fight for improved access to mental health resources and rights, it is crucial to remember that change does not happen overnight. It requires persistence, resilience, and a commitment to the cause. Advocacy is not always easy, but the rewards are immeasurable. By empowering individuals to advocate for mental health rights, we can create a society that values and supports the well-being of all its members.

So let's join forces, armed with knowledge, humor, and a passion for change. Let's raise our voices and advocate for improved access to mental health resources and rights. Together, we can make a difference and create a world where mental health is not just a priority but a fundamental right. As the saying goes, "If you want to go fast, go alone. If you want to go far, go together." Let's go far, together

:

Supporting Others With Bipolar Disorder

Offering Guidance and Resources for a Fulfilling Life

Living with bipolar disorder can be challenging, but with the right support and resources, individuals can thrive and lead fulfilling lives. In this segment of the book, we will explore how to provide guidance and resources to others living with bipolar disorder. Whether you are a friend, family member, or healthcare professional, your role in supporting someone with bipolar disorder is crucial. So, let's dive in and learn how to make a positive impact!

Understanding Bipolar Disorder:

Before offering support, it's important to have a solid understanding of bipolar disorder. Bipolar disorder is a mental health condition characterized by extreme mood swings, ranging from manic highs to depressive lows. These mood swings can disrupt daily life and relationships, making it essential to provide the right support.

1. Be an Active Listener:

One of the most powerful ways to support someone with bipolar disorder is by being an active listener. Allow them to express their thoughts, emotions, and concerns without judgment. Give them your undivided attention and validate their experiences. Remember, it's not about offering solutions but providing a safe space for them to be heard.

2. Educate Yourself:

To offer the best support, educate yourself about bipolar disorder. Read books, attend support groups, and seek information from reputable sources. By understanding the symptoms, treatment options, and challenges associated with bipolar disorder, you can provide informed guidance and resources.

3. Encourage Professional Help:

While your support is invaluable, it's crucial to encourage the individual to seek professional help. Bipolar disorder often requires a comprehensive treatment plan involving therapy, medication, and lifestyle adjustments. Be a source of encouragement and offer assistance in finding qualified healthcare professionals.

4. Foster a Supportive Network:

Supporting someone with bipolar disorder is not a one-person job. Encourage the individual to build a support network that includes family, friends, and support groups. Connecting with others who have similar experiences can provide a sense of community, understanding, and shared resources.

5. Promote Healthy Lifestyle Choices:

A healthy lifestyle plays a significant role in managing bipolar disorder. Encourage the individual to prioritize regular exercise, balanced nutrition, and sufficient sleep. Help them establish healthy routines and assist in finding activities they enjoy, such as yoga, hiking, or painting, as these can serve as therapeutic outlets.

6. Monitor Medication Compliance:

If the individual is taking medication to manage their bipolar disorder, it's important to support them in maintaining compliance. Offer reminders, assist with medication management tools, and be a sounding board for any concerns or side effects they may experience.

7. Help Identify Triggers and Warning Signs:

Bipolar disorder often has triggers and warning signs that can precede mood swings. Support the individual in identifying these triggers and warning signs, as early intervention can prevent or lessen the severity of episodes. Encourage them to keep a mood journal and establish coping strategies to manage these situations.

8. Celebrate Accomplishments:

Living with bipolar disorder is not easy, so it's important to celebrate every accomplishment, big or small. Acknowledge their efforts, resilience, and progress. Be their cheerleader, reminding them of how far they've come and inspiring them to keep moving forward.

Supporting others with bipolar disorder requires empathy, understanding, and a commitment to their well-being. By being an active listener, educating yourself, encouraging professional help, fostering a supportive network, promoting healthy lifestyle choices, monitoring medication compliance, helping identify triggers and warning signs, and celebrating accomplishments, you can make a significant positive impact on their journey towards a fulfilling life.

Remember, supporting someone with bipolar disorder is not about "fixing" them; it's about offering guidance, resources, and love. So, let's be there for them, cheer them on, and help them navigate the ups and downs of bipolar disorder with strength and resilience. Together, we can make a difference! And hey, remember to laugh along the way because humor is the best medicine, even when dealing with serious topics like bipolar disorder.

Bipolar Disorder and Gender Equality

Exploring the Intersection of Bipolar Disorder and Gender Equality, Advocating for Equal Treatment and Support

Chapter Title: Balancing the Scales: Bipolar Disorder and Gender Equality

Introduction:

In this chapter, we will delve into the fascinating and often overlooked connection between bipolar disorder and gender equality. While these two topics may seem unrelated at first glance, they intertwine in surprising and meaningful ways. We will explore the unique challenges faced by individuals with bipolar disorder, particularly women, and shed light on the importance of equal treatment and support for all genders. So, buckle up and get ready to dive into the complex world of bipolar disorder and gender equality!

Section 1: Understanding Bipolar Disorder

Let's start by unraveling the intricacies of bipolar disorder. Bipolar disorder is a mental health condition characterized by extreme mood swings, ranging from manic episodes of elevated energy and euphoria to depressive episodes of profound sadness and despair. These mood fluctuations can disrupt a person's daily life, relationships, and overall well-being. Understanding the symptoms, causes, and treatments of bipolar disorder is crucial to comprehending the challenges faced by individuals who navigate this rollercoaster ride.

Section 2: The Gendered Face of Bipolar Disorder

Did you know that bipolar disorder affects women differently than men? That's right, folks! Research suggests that hormonal fluctuations, such as those experienced during menstruation and pregnancy, can influence the severity and frequency of bipolar episodes in women. Furthermore, societal pressures, gender roles, and cultural expectations can exacerbate the challenges faced by women with bipolar disorder. It's time we shed light on these gendered aspects and work towards achieving gender equality in the realm of mental health.

Section 3: Advocating for Equal Treatment and Support

Now that we understand the unique intersection of bipolar disorder and gender equality, it's time to advocate for change. Our society has made significant strides in recognizing the importance of mental health, but we still have a long way to go. It's essential to ensure that individuals with bipolar disorder, regardless of gender, have access to equal treatment, support, and resources. We will explore strategies to promote gender equality in mental health care, debunk common misconceptions, and encourage open conversations about bipolar disorder.

Section 4: Sharing Stories, Changing Lives

Throughout this chapter, we will share stories of individuals who have thrived despite the challenges posed by bipolar disorder and gender inequality. Their experiences serve as a reminder that with the right treatment, support, and a dash of resilience, it is possible to live a fulfilling and meaningful life. These narratives will inspire and empower readers to advocate for their own well-being and the equal treatment of others.

Conclusion:

As we conclude this segment, let's remember that the journey towards gender equality in mental health is a collective effort. By exploring the intersection of bipolar disorder and gender equality, we have highlighted the need for change, understanding, and empathy. It's time to break down the barriers that hinder equal treatment and support, ensuring that everyone, regardless of their gender, can thrive amidst the ups and downs of bipolar disorder. So, let's join forces, raise awareness, and create a world that embraces and supports the mental well-being of all. After all, we're in this together!

Joke: Why did the bipolar person become a chef? Because they love to experience both the highs and lows of flavor!

Creating a Supportive Community

When it comes to living with bipolar disorder, one of the most crucial elements of managing and thriving is having a strong support system. Building a supportive community of individuals who understand what it's like to navigate the ups and downs of bipolar disorder can make all the difference in the world. It's like having a squad of superheroes by your side, ready to leap into action when you need them the most. So, let's dive into the importance of creating a supportive community and how to go about it.

First things first, let's address the elephant in the room - bipolar disorder can be tough. We all know it. But hey, life is all about finding the silver linings, right? And one of those silver linings is the opportunity to connect with others who are going through similar experiences. Trust me, there's nothing quite like bonding over mood swings and medication side effects to bring people together. It's like a secret club, except the membership fee is a little higher than your average book club.

Now, you may be wondering, how exactly does a supportive community help? Well, picture this: you're having a particularly rough day, feeling like you're riding an emotional rollercoaster with no brakes. Who do you turn to for support? Your mom? Your best friend? Well, those are great options, but having a community of individuals who truly understand what you're going through adds a whole new level of comfort and understanding.

In a supportive community, you can share your experiences, fears, and victories without fear of judgment. These are the people who get it, who understand the intricacies of bipolar disorder and can offer invaluable advice and empathy. They've been there, done that, and have the mood chart to prove it. Plus, let's be honest, who better to ask for tips on finding the perfect therapist or navigating the medication maze than someone who has been through it themselves?

Now, building a supportive community doesn't happen overnight. It takes time, effort, and a sprinkle of social skills. So, let's break it down into a few simple steps to get you started:

Step 1: Seek out support groups. These can be in-person or online, depending on your comfort level and location. Trust me, there's a group for everything these days – from early birds who want to conquer the world at 4 am to night owls who can't fall asleep until 4 am.

Step 2: Engage in conversations. Don't be afraid to share your story and ask questions. Remember, vulnerability is not a weakness, it's a superpower. Plus, you never know, you might just meet your bipolar BFF who shares your love for puns and penguins.

Step 3: Be an active participant. Don't just lurk in the shadows, like a ninja with a smartphone. Engage, offer support, and be the superhero you've always wanted to be. Remember, kindness and compassion are contagious.

Step 4: Take it offline. Once you've established connections online, why not take the leap and meet up in person? Grab a cup of coffee, go for a walk, or organize a pizza party. The possibilities are endless, just like your potential for building meaningful friendships.

And remember, in this supportive community, laughter is the best medicine. So, let's lighten the mood with a joke, shall we?

Why did the bipolar bear join the support group?

Because he heard they had great polar-ice cream socials!

Creating a supportive community of individuals with bipolar disorder is not just about finding people who understand your struggles, but also about building a network of love, laughter, and shared experiences. So, go out there, find your tribe, and together, let's thrive in the ups and downs of bipolar disorder!

Chapter 8: Conclusion

Reflecting on the Journey

As you turn the pages of this book, taking in the wealth of knowledge and experiences shared, it's important to take a moment to reflect on your own personal journey with bipolar disorder. This journey has been a rollercoaster ride, with its ups and downs, twists and turns. But through it all, you have grown and evolved into the resilient person you are today.

Reflecting on your journey allows you to acknowledge the progress you've made, the challenges you've overcome, and the strength you've discovered within yourself. It's a chance to celebrate your victories, no matter how small they may seem, and to give yourself credit for the hard work and determination it took to get where you are today.

Take a moment to close your eyes and think back to the beginning of your journey. Remember the confusion and fear you felt when you were first diagnosed. The uncertainty of what the future held, and the doubts that crept into your mind. But also remember the glimmers of hope that shone through, the support of loved ones, and the knowledge that you were not alone.

Now, fast forward to the present moment. Think about the progress you've made in managing your bipolar disorder. Perhaps you've found the right combination of medications that help stabilize your moods. Maybe you've developed coping mechanisms and strategies that allow you to navigate the ups and downs with more grace and ease. Or it could be that you've sought therapy and counseling, and have gained valuable insights and tools to manage your mental health.

No matter where you are in your journey, it's important to acknowledge and celebrate your growth. Bipolar disorder is not an easy road to travel, but you have shown incredible resilience and strength in facing the challenges that come with it. You are a warrior, and your journey is a testament to your courage and determination.

So, as you read through the pages of this book, take the time to reflect on your own personal journey. Pause after each chapter and ask yourself how the information and insights shared resonate with your own experiences. Take note of the progress you've made, the lessons you've learned, and the ways in which you have grown.

And remember, you are not alone on this journey. There are countless others who have walked, and continue to walk, the same path as you. Reach out for support when you need it, and offer support to others when you can. Together, we can thrive in the ups and downs of bipolar disorder, and live well despite the challenges we face.

Now, let's dive into the pages of this book and continue our journey of understanding, managing, and living well with bipolar disorder. But don't forget to pause every now and then, reflect on your own personal growth, and give yourself a pat on the back for how far you've come. And hey, remember, laughter is the best medicine, so don't forget to sprinkle in a few jokes along the way. After all, a little humor can go a long way in brightening even the darkest of days.

Moving Forward With Resilience

Final Thoughts on Leading a Fulfilling Life Despite the Challenges of Bipolar Disorder

Life is unpredictable, filled with highs and lows that can make it feel like a rollercoaster ride. But for those of us living with bipolar disorder, this ride can be even more intense, with twists and turns that can leave us feeling disoriented and overwhelmed. Yet, amidst the chaos, there is hope. In the face of bipolar disorder, resilience becomes our secret weapon, empowering us to move forward and lead fulfilling lives.

Resilience is not a magical quality that only a select few possess. It is a skill that can be cultivated and honed over time. Just like a muscle, the more we exercise resilience, the stronger it becomes. It is through resilience that we find the strength to persevere, to weather the storms that bipolar disorder may throw our way.

So how do we cultivate resilience? It starts with self-awareness. Understanding our triggers, our patterns, and our limits allows us to navigate the ups and downs with greater ease. It's like having a compass that guides us through the darkest of times, reminding us of our inner strength and ability to overcome.

But resilience is not just about weathering the storm; it's also about embracing the sunshine. It's about finding joy and fulfillment in the little moments, even amidst the challenges of bipolar disorder. It's about celebrating our victories, no matter how small they may seem. Whether it's getting out of bed on a difficult day or accomplishing a long-term goal, each step forward is a testament to our resilience.

One key aspect of leading a fulfilling life with bipolar disorder is the importance of support. We are not alone in this journey, and reaching out to others who understand can make a world of difference. Whether it's through therapy, support groups, or simply having a trusted friend or family member to lean on, having a strong support system can provide the foundation we need to move forward with resilience.

But resilience is not just about bouncing back; it's about bouncing forward. It's about embracing the challenges as opportunities for growth and transformation. It's about learning from our experiences and using them to become stronger, wiser, and more compassionate individuals.

Now, I could sit here and give you a laundry list of tips and techniques for cultivating resilience, but let's be honest, who wants to read that? Instead, let me share a joke with you.

Why did the bipolar woman bring a ladder to the bar? Because she was always looking for the highs!

Now, I know that living with bipolar disorder is no laughing matter, but sometimes a little humor can go a long way in lightening the load. Laughter is a form of resilience in itself, a reminder that even in the darkest of times, there is still lightness and joy to be found.

So, my friends, as we come to the end of this journey together, let us remember that resilience is not just about surviving; it's about thriving. It's about embracing the challenges, finding support, and never giving up. It's about living a life that is not defined by bipolar disorder, but by our strength, resilience, and ability to find joy amidst the ups and downs.

As we move forward with resilience, let us hold our heads high, knowing that we are capable of leading fulfilling lives despite the challenges we face. Let us embrace the journey, with all its twists and turns, and find solace in the fact that we are not alone. Together, we can move mountains and defy the odds.

So, my dear readers, go forth with resilience in your hearts and a smile on your face. The world is waiting for you to shine.

Continuing the Journey

After journeying through the ups and downs of bipolar disorder with me, you might be wondering, "Where do I go from here?" Well, fear not, my fellow bipolar women! While this book has provided you with a comprehensive guide to understanding, managing, and living well with bipolar disorder, there is still so much more to explore and learn on this ongoing journey.

First and foremost, it's crucial to recognize that this book is just the beginning. It's like the appetizer to a delicious feast of knowledge and support that awaits you. There are countless resources available to help you further navigate the complexities of bipolar disorder and continue your growth towards thriving in every aspect of your life.

One valuable resource that I highly recommend is support groups. These communities of individuals who understand firsthand the challenges of bipolar disorder can provide a safe space for you to share your experiences, seek advice, and find solace in the company of others who truly get it. Plus, you might even make some new friends along the way! Just be prepared for the occasional questionable potluck dish — we all have our culinary quirks.

Additionally, therapy is an essential tool for ongoing support and growth. A skilled therapist can help you navigate the emotional and psychological aspects of bipolar disorder, providing guidance and coping strategies tailored specifically to your unique needs. Think of them as your personal cheerleader, ready to help you tackle any hurdles that may come your way. And remember, therapy doesn't have to be all serious and somber — a good therapist knows how to sprinkle a little humor into the mix to lighten the mood.

In the realm of self-help literature, there is a plethora of books out there that can provide further insights and practical strategies for managing bipolar disorder. From memoirs by individuals who have triumphed over their own struggles to workbooks that offer exercises and tools for self-reflection, there is something for everyone. Just be warned, some of these books may be as thick as a phone book — but don't worry, they're much more interesting!

For those who prefer a more modern approach, technology has opened up a world of possibilities. There are numerous apps available that can help you track your moods, manage medication schedules, and even provide guided meditations and relaxation exercises. It's like having a pocket-sized therapist right at your fingertips — although I must admit, they're not great at giving high fives.

And finally, never underestimate the power of a strong support system. Surround yourself with friends and family who understand and accept you, quirks and all. These are the people who will be there for you through the highs and lows, providing a shoulder to lean on and a listening ear. And hey, they might even bring you a latte when you're feeling particularly down — now that's true friendship.

So my dear bipolar women, as you continue your journey beyond the pages of this book, remember that there is a world of resources and support waiting for you. Embrace the opportunities to learn, grow, and connect with others who share your experiences. And most importantly, never forget to laugh along the way — after all, humor is the best medicine, right? Now go forth, my fellow thrivers, and conquer the world with your resilient spirit and infectious laughter!

Acknowledgments

Writing a book is a labor of love, but it's not a solitary endeavor. Behind every successful book, there is a team of dedicated individuals who have contributed their time, expertise, and support. These unsung heroes are the ones we want to acknowledge and express our deepest gratitude to.

First and foremost, we would like to thank our readers. Your unwavering support and enthusiasm for our work have been a constant source of inspiration. Your feedback and encouragement have pushed us to delve deeper into the subject matter and provide you with the most comprehensive guide possible. We are grateful for your trust in us and for joining us on this journey.

To our editor, Sarah, you have been our guiding light throughout the entire process. Your keen eye for detail and your unwavering commitment to excellence have transformed our words into a polished and impactful manuscript. Your feedback and suggestions have helped shape the book into what it is today. We are forever indebted to you for your expertise and dedication.

We would also like to extend our gratitude to our cover designer, Alex. Your creativity and talent have given our book a visually stunning cover that captures the essence of our message. Your ability to translate our vision into a work of art is truly remarkable.

To our research assistant, Mark, thank you for tirelessly scouring through countless articles, studies, and books to provide us with the most up-to-date and accurate information. Your meticulousness and dedication to thorough research have been invaluable in ensuring the accuracy and credibility of our work.

A special mention goes to our friends and family who have supported us throughout this journey. Your unwavering belief in our abilities and your constant words of encouragement have kept us going during the challenging times. Thank you for understanding when we had to cancel plans or disappear for days on end to meet deadlines. Your love and support mean the world to us.

Last but certainly not least, we want to express our heartfelt appreciation to the individuals who have shared their personal stories and experiences with bipolar disorder. Your courage and vulnerability in opening up about your struggles and triumphs have provided invaluable insights and perspectives. Your stories have given this book a human touch, making it relatable and meaningful to readers who may be going through similar experiences.

In conclusion, the creation and publication of this book would not have been possible without the contributions of these amazing individuals. We are eternally grateful for their support, expertise, and unwavering belief in our work. To all those mentioned and those who may not have been, thank you from the bottom of our hearts. You have made this journey worthwhile, and we hope that our book will make a positive impact on the lives of those who read it.

And now, for a little joke to lighten the mood. Why did the book go to therapy? Because it had too many characters! Thank you for indulging us.

About the Author

In the pages of "Bipolar Women: Thriving in the Ups and Downs," you'll find an invaluable guide to understanding, managing, and living well with bipolar disorder. But before we delve into the rich tapestry of insights and strategies within these pages, let's take a moment to meet the brilliant mind behind this transformative work.

Our author, let's call her Sarah, is no stranger to the challenges of bipolar disorder. In fact, she's intimately acquainted with the rollercoaster of emotions, the dizzying highs, and the crushing lows that come with this often misunderstood condition. Sarah's personal experience with bipolar disorder forms the foundation of her expertise, providing a unique perspective that is both relatable and enlightening.

Raised in a small town with big dreams, Sarah was a force to be reckoned with from an early age. She excelled academically, always hungry for knowledge and eager to unravel the complexities of the human mind. Little did she know that her own mind held secrets waiting to be unlocked.

As she navigated her teenage years, Sarah found herself grappling with an array of emotions that seemed to have a life of their own. One day, she would soar through the sky, bursting with creativity and energy, ready to conquer the world. The next, she would find herself sinking into a dark abyss, plagued by sadness and despair. It was during these tumultuous times that she discovered the name for her experiences - bipolar disorder.

Determined to take control of her own narrative, Sarah embarked on a journey of self-discovery and healing. She devoured books, attended therapy sessions, and sought out support groups. Through trial and error, she developed coping mechanisms, honed her management skills, and discovered a resilience within herself that she never knew existed.

But Sarah's journey didn't end there. Instead of keeping her newfound wisdom to herself, she made it her mission to share her experiences and knowledge with others. Recognizing the lack of resources specifically tailored to women with bipolar disorder, she decided to write the book she wished she had when she was first diagnosed.

And so, "Bipolar Women: Thriving in the Ups and Downs" was born. Within its pages, Sarah combines her personal anecdotes, clinical research, and expert advice to create a comprehensive guide that empowers women to not just survive, but thrive with bipolar disorder. She tackles everything from managing medications and building a support network to navigating relationships and harnessing creativity. With a touch of humor and a generous sprinkling of wisdom, Sarah brings a ray of hope to every woman who has ever felt lost in the labyrinth of bipolar disorder.

Now, as you embark on your own journey through these pages, remember that you are not alone. Sarah's story, and the stories of countless other women who have battled bipolar disorder, are here to remind you that you have the strength within you to conquer anything that comes your way. So buckle up, my friends, and get ready for an adventure like no other. Let's dive into the wild and wonderful world of bipolar disorder, where the ups and downs may be challenging, but the rewards are immeasurable.

Remember, if life hands you lemons, squeeze them into your iced tea and laugh in the face of adversity. After all, humor is the best medicine. And with Sarah as your guide, you'll be laughing your way to a brighter tomorrow in no time.

So without further ado, let's turn the page and begin this extraordinary journey together. Welcome to the world of "Bipolar Women: Thriving in the Ups and Downs" -- where understanding, managing, and living well with bipolar disorder is not just a possibility, but a reality waiting to be embraced.